T0194159

CROSSRUPTION
THE JOURNEY OF A DISRUPTED LIFE

JACOB WILLIAM
WITH ROBERT NOLAND

WESTBOW
PRESS®
A DIVISION OF THOMAS NELSON
& ZONDERVAN

WestBow Press books may be ordered through booksellers or by contacting:

WestBow Press
A Division of Thomas Nelson & Zondervan
1663 Liberty Drive
Bloomington, IN 47403
www.westbowpress.com
1 (866) 928-1240

Scripture quotations marked (NIV) are taken from the Holy Bible, New International Version®, NIV®. Copyright © 1973, 1978, 1984, 2011 by Biblica, Inc.™ Used by permission of Zondervan. All rights reserved worldwide.

Scripture quotations taken from the New American Standard Bible® (NASB), Copyright © 1960, 1962, 1963, 1968, 1971, 1972, 1973, 1975, 1977, 1995 by The Lockman Foundation Used by permission.

Scripture quotations are taken from the Holy Bible, New Living Translation, copyright ©1996, 2004, 2007, 2013, 2015 by Tyndale House Foundation. Used by permission of Tyndale House Publishers, Inc., Carol Stream, Illinois 60188. All rights reserved.

Scripture quotations taken from the Amplified® Bible (AMP), Copyright © 2015 by The Lockman Foundation Used by permission.

Scripture quotations taken from the Amplified® Bible (AMPC), Copyright © 1954, 1958, 1962, 1964, 1965, 1987 by The Lockman Foundation Used by permission.

Scripture quotations marked MSG are taken from THE MESSAGE, copyright © 1993, 1994, 1995, 1996, 2000, 2001, 2002 by Eugene H. Peterson. Used by permission of NavPress. All rights reserved. Represented by Tyndale House Publishers, Inc.

The author has italicized or bolded text in Scripture quotations for emphasis.

ISBN: 978-1-5127-8736-8 (sc)
ISBN: 978-1-5127-8738-2 (hc)
ISBN: 978-1-5127-8737-5 (e)

Library of Congress Control Number: 2017907281

Print information available on the last page.

WestBow Press rev. date: 09/22/2017

Contents

Acknowledgments

Crossruption is a journey, and journeys are never traveled alone. My own, thus far, has included the people on this page, to whom I am grateful.

Dad and Mom got me started on this journey, living lives of sacrifice and providing me with a foundation of unconditional love.

My wife and my children tried to see what I was seeing, believed, and stood by me through all the challenges, doubts, and frustrations while experiencing the joy of seeing God move in our lives. My family continually encouraged me to persevere and complete this book.

My brother brought the God perspective to our home. (How I hated that in the early stages of my life!) And the members of his family have played God-ordained roles.

My grandparents from both sides of the family, the late Dr. and Mrs. J. S. William and the late Mr. and Mrs. P. C. Varghese, have been foundational in weaving the God paradigm within our families.

My extended family—uncles, aunts, and cousins—have helped shape my career and my life.

My college mates in Allahabad, India, were truly "iron sharpening iron" with a special mention of P.C. Varghese and Jonathan Maraj, staff of Union of Evangelical Students of India, who worked tirelessly among the students to lay a biblical foundation.

My business partners have been a steadfast support. Without them, this book would not have been born.

My business associates showed me the reality of whom I was inside and set me on a quest to bridge my hypocrisy.

My friends in Concord, North Carolina, were indispensable in connecting the dots of this journey.

Robert Noland instantly saw the message of this book in another dimension and took on the challenge of working with a businessman who had written a book on spirituality. Without his editing skills, this manuscript would never have seen the light of day.

Amy Balamut created the logo that well reflects the core message of the book.

The Frame of Mind team in India produced incredible videos to communicate concepts in simple terms.

Don Dartt, Amick Cutler, KC Clark, Rick Hoganson, and the team at Louder Agency all brought their A-game to help get the word out about *Crossruption*.

Finally, I am grateful to the countless number of people who have and will join us on this journey of *Crossruption*!

Part I

Introduction

A religion of mere emotion and sensationalism is the most terrible of all curses that can come upon any people. The absence of reality is sad enough, but the aggravation of pretense is a deadly sin. (Samuel Chadwick, 1860–1932)

Interruption and Innovation

Three stories. Three companies. Same results.

The Internet was relatively new. People understood shopping only as a brick-and-mortar experience. You went, you found, you bought, and you took home. Enter Amazon. You could order anything from baby wipes to books and never get out of your pajamas—a one-stop shop in the palm of your hand. Then the products showed up at your door. Retail faced disruption. The way we view purchasing products and services was changed forever.

Over many decades, the music industry made countless millionaires. People involved in this business led charmed lives. But as new technology began to take hold, free Internet file sharing started hurting the record labels. Enter Apple. You could buy the digital download of one single song and didn't have to purchase an album. No inventory. Disruption had come to a long-static industry, bringing transformation along kicking and screaming. The way we purchase and access music was changed forever.

Since the automobile became the norm in the world of transportation, the taxicab had a monopoly on pay-per-ride service in any city. For many decades, no other option was even considered. Not even carpooling or ridesharing caught on culturally. Enter Uber. Ordinary people turned their private cars into public cabs. A long-standing monopoly was challenged. Those in major cities who would never set foot in a cab now accessed the Uber app each day. The transportation industry was changed forever.

Disruptive innovation is a term coined by Clayton Christensen to describe the process by which a product or service takes root, initially in simple applications at the bottom of a market, providing less-than-ideal solutions, and then relentlessly moving up the value chain, eventually displacing established competitors.

Today, disruption in the market has become commonplace. As consumers, we now expect these shake-ups. We anticipate them and want them to take place, because we have come to believe that disruptions in the delivery of products and services ultimately make our lives better. The disruptors of commerce are the entities that forever:

- Challenge the status quo
- Change their industries
- Champion a new trail for the world to follow

Disruption displaces and replaces the old with the new, starting as insignificant change, becoming significant, and finally dominating. Whether you are a financier or a farmer, on welfare or on Wall Street, living in the First World or the Third World or in between, you are experiencing the impact of global economic disruption.

As a serial entrepreneur seeking to thrive in this environment, I continually recognize that if my businesses are not moving forward, they are slipping backward. Like a plant that is either growing or dying, a business has no safe and static position—ever. There is no possibility of hibernation in the business world. Over the past fifteen years, my business partners and I have consistently made strategic decisions that have allowed our company to grow globally amid epic changes in the world's commerce. The next decade will see a radical transformation in every area of life on a scale unmatched throughout the last century. Progress in all fields will be rapid and phenomenal. We are living in an exciting time!

But what about the pioneers who blaze the trail and drive the demand, and the people who take advantage of this innovation in commerce? A deep chasm is rapidly developing. Even as we have grown accustomed to market disruption and tremendous economic growth, we have developed a systemic personal identity problem. We know what we do and we know what we have, but we do not know who we are, because we define ourselves by what we do and what we have.

While we have been extremely successful at innovation, we have also failed by allowing our products, services, and achievements to define our personal identities. We have been amazing at producing disruption in the marketplace but have become enslaved to our own creations.

Since the first people walked the earth, human beings have demanded an answer to the question of personal identity. We all ask, "Who am I?" and typically answer philosophically in the mind and materially in terms of the body. Therefore, we live in a time when we define ourselves by:

+ What we do
+ What we think
+ What we believe
+ How we feel
+ What we possess
+ Where we live
+ What others do
+ What others think of us

Today, most people define their identities by a mix of all these factors. The number of "likes," "shares," and "followers" is progressively becoming the prime driver of personal identity.

There is nothing wrong with achievement and all of its implications, because this can bring rich meaning to life. Self-expression through success can create a beautiful painting of humanity. However, we seem to have forgotten that the painting does not *define* the painter but merely *expresses* the painter. Consider these deep inner dilemmas:

- If I define myself by what I *do*, what if I lose that position or my ability to perform?
- If I define myself by how I *feel*, what if my frame of mind markedly changes?
- If I define myself by what I *possess*, what if I lose my resources and must give up what I own?
- If I define myself by where I *live*, what if I must relocate or a natural disaster displaces me?
- If I define myself by what others *think* of me, what if the people in my circle constantly disapprove of or disagree with me?

All these definitions of identification revolve around variables that too easily change and therefore constantly redefine who we are. But a dog is not a dog because it barks; instead, it barks because it is a dog. External variables do not define an internal constant, but an internal constant defines all external variables.

Our definitions of personal identity have progressively and subconsciously become so restricted by doing, feeling, possessing, and other extrinsic expressions that we have lost the intrinsic understanding of who we are. Foundational lines that separate our actions and feelings from our inner beings have been blurred.

So what does this discussion of disruption in the marketplace have to do with our twenty-first-century identity crisis? Everything!

The Cosmic Vacuum

While our world constantly changes around us, we stay the same, mired in our internal emptiness; the greater the external progression, the greater the internal regression.

What is the point of technological and economic progress if we do not know how to live at peace with ourselves and in community with one another? We have the greatest invisible technology networks in history connecting us but are visibly divided like never before. We are united through the Internet yet separated by skin color, abstract beliefs of religion, and geographical loyalties. What a paradox! Is this really the life we dreamed of and want to leave as a legacy to the next generation?

When we work and achieve all we want but are still empty inside, we think new things, relationships, and substances will make us happy, but when our expectations are not met, this creates conflict and disappointment. In extreme cases, the resulting imbalances in the brain can lead to all sorts of physical and mental abuse.

We have one group of people who have achieved possession and fame. The people who have "made it" realize their celebrity status and success will not fill the inner cosmic vacuum. This is one of the most horrifying feelings—to have everything a human being could need physically and intellectually but still have an inner sense of emptiness that words cannot express. The greatest pain for an individual is not the lack of things, but the lack of inner peace in the midst of wealth and fame. Inner conflict in the midst of intellectual and physical abundance is a suffering that humanity is not wired to handle.

Then there is the group desperately trying to either mimic or reach the level of the "rich and famous," thinking it is the things and possessions of life that bring true satisfaction. Such is the paradox of life.

The cosmic vacuum in an individual is that sense of inner emptiness irrespective of wealth or poverty; the conscious awareness that "there must be more to life than this."

The many celebrities who die tragically despite wealth and fame show the depth of our society's problems. Those who bring great joy, laughter, and inspiration to millions cry out desperately on the inside—depressed, isolated, and alone. This is the life of far too many today.

We have everything we need on the outside but are bankrupt on the inside. We wear the finest clothing and have the latest devices, all the while feeling naked and empty. We eat and drink to excess but starve and thirst on the inside.

The common denominator that binds all humanity together—rich or poor, young or old—is the emptiness that haunts us when we are alone. We are the only beings on earth that can be desperately lonely in the midst of a crowd. We long for authentic relationships, so we work for more "likes" and "followers" to fill the cosmic black hole inside us.

We all chase mirages as we grow up. We start by saying, "If only I was in middle school." Then, once in middle school, the vicious cycle continues as we lament:

+ If only I was in high school
+ If only I was in college
+ If only I had a boyfriend or girlfriend
+ If only I had a great job
+ If only I had a home
+ If only I had a bigger home
+ If only I had fame and success
+ If only I had significance

We chase this illusion of "if only" our entire lives, never realizing when we finally reach our mythical goal that the mirage has moved ahead to the next spot. We might well end our lives by saying, "If only I hadn't chased the 'if onlys'!"

This aspect of human behavior creates a divided life.

Picture a waffle. Imagine the grid of perfect squares—five up and four across, twenty total. You want to pour syrup onto your waffle, but you want to keep the compartments separate—nothing touching or intermingling. So you try to pour the syrup into each tiny square without any overflow. How hard would that be? How tricky would controlling the flow be? How difficult and time consuming would it be to pour syrup onto a waffle this way?

While this may sound ridiculous, many of us do the same thing with our lives, filling the compartments one at a time and working to keep them all separate.

We human beings have the unique ability to mask our internal reality with a very different external appearance, but we are still left with an emptiness and longing to bridge the gap between who we truly are and who we portray ourselves to be.

The public sees a businessman wearing Armani suits, driving a Mercedes, eating at five-star restaurants, and living in a mansion, but his personal life is bankrupt.

A beautiful fashion model, adored by millions, suffers from low self-esteem and is constantly fighting on the inside to maintain her external image. Women want to "be her," but she wants to become someone else. The public perception is not at all an accurate reflection of her true inner state.

We may think that what we possess allows for a powerful identity. However, all of our actions, possessions, and achievements put together will not satisfy our innermost desire for something more.

Our culture breeds the illusion that life's trappings are enough. No wonder this illusion influences our belief systems so strongly.

WRESTLING WITH RELIGION

Our technology and gadgets are progressively creating a virtual and impersonal social media environment, while our desire for relationship goes far beyond and vastly deeper than our current digital environment. We have a hardwired need for personal intimacy and communion at a level beyond the mind and body.

In our evolutionary worldview, we think sex, regardless of the context, will solve the problem. While we can certainly feel satisfaction for a few fleeting moments, those feelings are always a temporary solution. When the act is finished, the same nagging emptiness slowly returns and, for many, the depth of loneliness only increases. We keep seeking wilder adventures, yet none of them will end the inner conflict.

Taking a materialistic approach, we decide possessions will solve the problem, but new and better products will never end our maddening pursuit of this mirage.

In our philosophical worldview, we may think achievement will solve the problem and desperately seek intellectual solutions to our relational dilemma. We could find convincing proof for the Big Bang or Darwin's theory of the origin of mankind yet still not fill our emptiness. Whether or not we believe in a creator, whether we think we came from monkeys or gods, the right understanding of the origin of life won't fulfill our deep need for a relationship that goes beyond the mind and body.

Mankind created religion as the answer to this innate spiritual relational need that humanity is hardwired to experience. A god up in the air, a god somewhere inside us, a god everywhere around us, amounts only to what Karl Marx called the "opium of the people."

Long ago, some very intelligent people realized that nothing in the body or the mind meets our relational needs, so they introduced the worst possible answer to inner human longing: we should try to find God—as if He is the One who is lost and needs to be found! For our purposes in this book, we will call this mindset "religion."

Therefore, religion:

+ Fools people into thinking they have their spiritual and relational problems solved by doing a set of actions or going to certain "spiritual" locations
+ Attempts to fill humanity's spiritual vacuum through gaining intellectual information about God
+ Creates names, images, and rules by which to live
+ Acknowledges supernatural reality only through the mind

In creating religion, people defined what any god looked like and what this god would want them to do and not do. These rules came from the moral do's and don'ts ingrained in us. The more people adhered to this belief system, the more religious they understood themselves to be and the more religious they appeared to be to others.

Religion in the twenty-first century has become a new business model, but one that is recession proof because, just like health and food, spiritual hunger is a constant need.

Mankind's manipulating of the conscious and subconscious mind was an attempt to answer these questions:

+ Who am I?
+ Where did I come from?
+ Why am I here?
+ Where am I going?

The spirituality of religion is affirmed by external activity; while the inner core of religion is belief, the outer shell is behavior. If you must give evidence for your religious identity, it does not matter whether you are

Christian, Hindu, Muslim, or an atheist. Whatever religion you espouse, the evidence is based upon the same formula: "I believe, and I behave according to my beliefs." The expressions of all religions depend on circumstance and location. In today's Western-influenced culture, the evidence for all religions contain four elements:

+ Belief (thought, the mind)
+ Behavior (action, the body)
+ Circumstance (reaction to the surrounding environment)
+ Location (a person's specific current setting)

I spent my childhood and early adult life in India. While the Christian church has been active there for centuries, less than 3 percent of the people identify themselves as Christian. I was raised in a Christian home, as was my wife. We saw that the tenets of Hinduism and Islam had a strong influence on every facet of Indian society. When you grow up surrounded by religion, identifying the characteristics of religion becomes easy.

THE RELIGION OF HINDUISM

For Hindus, beliefs and behaviors define how religious you are. Hindus believe in:

+ Karma (the law of cause and effect, determining individual destiny by thoughts, words, and deeds)
+ Temple worship
+ Reading holy books to gain knowledge
+ Rituals
+ Sacraments
+ Personal devotions
+ Personal growth through discipline
+ Fighting over denominational differences
+ Moral behavior
+ Purification
+ Pilgrimage

+ Charity work
+ Evangelism to promote belief and behavior
+ Self-inquiry and examination
+ Meditation
+ Complete surrender

All these elements will help the Hindu gain knowledge of:

+ Truth within
+ A pinnacle of consciousness (emotions) to become one with God
+ God Himself
+ God in holy places

The core of Hinduism is belief, good practice, and the expression of godly ideals. However, these practices and expressions are based on individual convenience.

Salvation in Hinduism depends on good deeds, obtained by visiting holy places and performing holy rituals. The mind and body reach out to the spiritual, but the spiritual is just a belief of the mind with no interconnection between the spiritual and the mind of the individual. A dip in the river Ganges and a visit to Sabarimala, accompanied by behavioral rituals, assures you of salvation. What you believe and what you do determines salvation. The fundamental tenet of Hinduism is to believe and behave so that God will bring good to you.

The Religion of Islam

While Hinduism is the predominant religion in my native India, the nation is home to the second-largest Muslim population in the world.

Muslims believe in:

+ One supreme God, Allah, who has ninety-nine attributes
+ Reading the Qur'an to gain knowledge about what Allah wants
+ Worshiping Allah alone
+ Obeying all of Allah's commandments

+ Salvation through both belief and practice
+ Allah as the judge with perfect justice, according to each person's actions
+ The righteous life of good deeds that brings paradise (*jannah*)
+ Hellfire (*jahannam*) where unbelievers will be punished
+ Shariah as the divine code of practice and guidance
+ Fighting over denominational differences
+ Holding to the five pillars or commitments: the declaration of faith, prayer, fasting, charity, and pilgrimage
+ Working for God
+ Expressing belief
+ Salvation after death
+ The core of Islam being belief, good practice, and religious expression based on individual convenience
+ What you believe and what you do as defining who you are

Salvation in Islam depends on good deeds, obtained by going to holy places and carrying out holy rituals. The mind and body work for Allah. There is absolutely no inter-connection between the visible and the invisible dimensions. A visit to Mecca accompanied by behavioral rituals assures you of salvation. Muslims believe that if they do certain things and visit certain places, they will go to paradise.

The fundamental tenet of Islam is to believe and behave so that God will bring good to you.

THE RELIGION OF BUDDHISM

Although only 6 percent of the world's people claim Buddhism as their religion, this belief system has gained popularity in the West, though its origins are in India. Many have adopted its general philosophy and follow the beliefs in loose, self-prescribed ways—an approach the religion itself encourages.

At its core, Buddhism emphasizes:

+ Living a moral life
+ Careful attention to thoughts, actions, wisdom, and understanding

- That suffering comes from unmet cravings and aversions
- That happiness is gained by giving up those cravings and aversions
- That the Eightfold Path can end suffering, focusing on moral actions, a keen awareness of thought life, and wisdom obtained through developing compassion for others
- Karma, which stresses that good and bad actions bring corresponding good and bad results
- That answers to problems lie inside us, not in anything or anyone on the outside

The core of Buddhism is belief and good practice, with an extreme emphasis on circumstance, location, and individual convenience. What you believe and what you do define who you are. Spirituality is a practice of the mind and body.

The fundamental tenets of Buddhism are to believe and behave.

THE RELIGION CALLED CHRISTIANITY

The followers of Christianity:

- Regularly gather at a religious location
- Read the Bible to gain knowledge of God and know what He expects them to do
- Sing songs
- Hear teaching
- Pray together
- Give of their resources—money and time
- Take part in worship, fellowship, and activities
- Fight over denominational differences
- Gain a sense of satisfaction through community
- Hope that when they die, their practice of belief will get them to Heaven

Salvation depends not on good deeds or visiting holy places and performing holy rituals, but on believing in Jesus and saying the sinner's prayer. Christians quote the Bible, believing that verbal confession of Jesus as Lord provides salvation. They believe in the spiritual, the interdimensional connection between the spirit and the mind, along with many more beliefs that have no present daily implications. Affirming the right beliefs is extremely fundamental in the religion called Christianity with specific activities to do that reflect that belief. The ticket to Heaven is based on an expression of belief and a confession of Jesus Christ that promises a future paradise with no apparent present consequences.

So What's the Difference?

As you can see by our comparison, Hinduism, Islam, Buddhism, and Christianity share many core principles, so here's a pivotal question: What then separates today's Christian from a Hindu, Muslim, or Buddhist? Today's brand of Christianity can appear to be no different from the other religions described above.

The genuineness of a person's Christianity is judged by what they believe and how closely they follow the culturally accepted belief system. The more active a person is in Christian organizations, the more spiritual that person is considered to be. Christianity is measured primarily based on good behavior, church attendance, and participation in spiritual activities. All too often, we feel good about what we do and then return to our self-centered, self-satisfied lives, expecting that when we die, we'll go to Heaven because we believe in Jesus and have done the right things.

For several years, the postmillennial and post-Christian generation have been asking crucial questions about Christian spiritual identity such as the following:

+ Why do the teachings of the Bible and the lifestyles of Christians seem incompatible?
+ Why is it when the law of the land concerning the Bible changes, the theology of Christians regarding the Bible also follows suit and changes?
+ When was the divorce between belief and behavior?

+ When did a strange remarriage of belief and behavior then take place for all the wrong reasons?

A generation is turning away from the faith because the mask is falling off so many Christians. We live at a time when truth is challenged on one end and manipulated on the other. Never in the history of Christianity have we heard so much talk and seen so much activity while people actually experience so little of Jesus.

The challenge is not so much the increase of evil but a stifling lack of truth. At the heart of all these systemic issues lies the greatest threat—a clear lack of Christian identity. The black and white of Scripture has degenerated into a hazy gray gleaned from culture.

We have separated the faith into liberal and conservative Christianity, because we now define our identity only according to actions or expressions. For many, this is what Christian religion is all about.

The religion of Christianity exists:

+ Where Christian identity is judged fundamentally by belief and its corresponding level of activity, with what people do and say as the focus.
+ When Jesus is promoted for people to be saved from hell.
+ When salvation becomes the *primary* purpose of Jesus.

Jesus did not come *just* to save mankind from going to hell.

Twenty-first-century believers in Jesus are very similar to the Pharisees in Jesus' day that believed in Jehovah. Both define their identities by what they do or do not do. Faith is affirmed by actions where more involvement means more faith.

Religion is not only mankind-centric but also God-centric. We often seek God for what He does, not for who He is. Twenty-first-century Christianity is all about what Jesus will do for us. Remember our earlier discussion of the disruptive products and services we have come to love? For many of us, Jesus has become another of those—used primarily on Sunday mornings and in a crisis. He ranks right up there with the newest smartphone for convenience and customer satisfaction.

Consider these statements:

+ We seek God for what He does.
+ We evaluate our relationship with God by what we do for Him.
+ We evaluate the relationships others have with God by what they do for Him.
+ We define God's identity by what He does.
+ We define our own identities by what we do, and define others by what they do.
+ God's activity for people and their activity for God are at the epicenter of all religion.

We must realize the version of Christianity we have created in the West—which is also poisoning all those who copy us in other parts of the world—is not a relational life disruption at all but rather a distortion of what Jesus lived and died to transform us into.

CHRISTIANITY AT A CROSSROADS

We have integrated Hollywood, Wall Street, and Silicon Valley into twenty-first-century Christianity. We have essentially made Jesus into a fantasy character in a great story. For some, He is a historical figure, while for others He is just a folk hero. Regardless, His story is sure to please because it is not only about good defeating evil but also about how He can help us when we are in trouble, rescuing us from the storms of life. He lives solely to solve our problems. This Jesus we have created is the ultimate Superman, the cowboy in a white hat, a wish-granting genie, and a bullet-dodging action hero straight from our favorite movies—all rolled into one. No wonder around 80 percent of Americans consistently say they believe in Him! Who wouldn't want such a hero? (But we must remember that the Bible in James 2:19 says 100 percent of demons believe in Jesus too.)

Today's Christianity is not about what this Superhero can do in us, but what He can do for us and what we should do for Him in return. We will do things for this Superman to stay in His good graces, because we want Him to do things for us, to save us when we're in trouble. We have fine-tuned our faith until it is an example of efficient product management.

The religion of Christianity is a perfect example of what is known in the business world as outsourcing. This is the process of finding a suitable external vendor to handle the aspects of a company that they either can't manage or choose to delegate.

I came to realize that I was involved in a religion that offered a product called God. I had outsourced its production to an enterprise network called the church where events were staged every week. This was a Christianity that fit my business lifestyle and gave me the illusion of being Heaven-bound for the bargain price of only 10 percent of my income.

I had outsourced my:

- Evangelism (sharing my faith) to the missions committee and those with that gift
- World outreach to full-time missionaries
- Ministry to my neighbors to the committee handling community hospitality
- Responsibility as a parent to the children's or student ministry
- Personal Bible study to my pastor or group leader

I was paying people to do my religion for me, because my time was too valuable and my life was too busy for a real personal relationship with God. I was told that simply believing in Jesus and trying to behave like Jesus out of gratitude was the guaranteed ticket to Heaven. The church measured my belief and behavior while forgetting that I could be someone on the inside and do something completely different on the outside. The metrics used were not my personal transformation from relational inner intimacy with the Father, but rather outer behavior.

Today's worship services involve music, dancing, drama, and lots of applause directed toward those on the stage. The result is an amazed audience, people who are happy to come week after week and dream that they are all bound for Heaven. We have created a product called Christianity that people will pay to experience. The Superman Jesus is a great character because He is distant from us but can be called upon anytime solely for our personal benefit.

Christianity today has been packaged to align well with Buddha in the expression of universal grace, love, and mercy, but is the message presented really any different from those of Pandit Ravishankar or Deepak Chopra?

Actually, Ravishankar does a better job of explaining unity, love, and hope than many pastors and priests do. Chopra does a better job of explaining the reality of the inner person. The church is competing with people who preach and practice the principles of the inner spirit better than most Christian leaders do.

As a result, today's Christianity is swiftly losing the precepts that differentiate it from other philosophies and religions. We go to church as if we were attending an Apple event—waiting for the next big thing to be revealed to help our lives.

Here is the problem: We know our inner emptiness, our desire for something more, will not be filled by anything the body, mind, or religion—even the religion of Christianity—offers.

So is there a solution? Can we find personal identity and self-worth in something other than ever-changing fashions, appetites, emotions, religious activity, and circumstances?

Is it possible to:

+ Take part in the divine nature of God Himself while we are here on earth?
+ Go beyond the weekly emotional ride or intellectual understanding of God and get into the beautiful balance where there is an incredible interplay of the spirit, mind, and body?
+ Have an inner constant in the midst of external variables?
+ Experience God Himself inside of us where we do not go to a temple to find God but we become the Temple of God?
+ Have everything in life but not be defined by those things or have nothing in life but not be defined by the lack of those things?
+ Live a life that goes against the law of the land that now contradicts the law of God?
+ Be transformed in our mind so our behavior transformation is an effect of internal transformation?
+ Have the mind of Christ where we overcome temptations just as He did?
+ Break down the racial barriers that divide us and find a common identity that unites us?

+ Love one another for who we are and not for the color of our skin or the nation in which we live?
+ *Become* like Jesus instead of merely *talking* about Jesus?

We can, but only by realizing and understanding that the demands of behavior in all religions are incredibly intelligent creations of mankind and do not have any spiritual tranformational impact in us. This transformation will come only by personally understanding that:

+ What we believe is not who we are
+ What we do is not who we are
+ What we achieve is not who we are
+ What we think is not who we are
+ What we feel is not who we are

A historical event occurred where God became man, was insulted by the religious system, suffered at their hands, was accused of blasphemy, was hung on a cross as a criminal, and rose again so He may have a personal relationship with humanity in humanity. This is not simply some belief statement but a transformational journey we are called to experience as a *consequence* of that belief. This historical event can become a present reality, where the power of the cross takes us on the journey called *Crossruption*.

THE DISRUPTED LIFE

Three stories. Three men. Same results.

The first man was an outcast from society. Rejected by his family and falsely accused of attempted rape, he languished in a foreign prison. While incarcerated, he came to the aid of a cellmate who happened to be a government employee. He asked that, upon the man's release, he put in a good word for him with the authorities. But the cellmate didn't keep his promise. For years the man waited in jail. When he was finally released, he went on to become the second-in-command of a kingdom and save his homeland from starvation, including his own brothers who had sold him into slavery.

Prison to palace. What happened?

The second man was an adopted son who led a life of privilege. But he had a bad temper. Witnessing a communal clash, he stepped in and killed someone from the opposing group. Fearing arrest, this murderer fled the country and created a new life for himself as a shepherd. Though he planned to live out the rest of his days in obscurity, he became the deliverer of his nation.

Lawbreaker to liberator. What happened?

The third man was a well-educated Pharisee, righteous to a fault and zealous to protect the Jewish law at all costs. He viewed Jesus' disciples as threats to his way of life and his beliefs, so under the authority of the teachers of the law, he set out to kill these followers. Traveling on his mission, he was struck blind by a powerful force invisible to others in his party. Given divine instructions to go to Damascus, he was led there to wait. This same man went on to write the bulk of the New Testament.

Terrorist to teacher. What happened?

The common thread in the lives of these men is that they were transformed to be defined not by what happened *through* them, but by what happened *in* them—not by what they possessed but by who possessed them, not by where they went but by who they followed, not by where they lived but by who lived within them.

The life disruption they experienced transformed their identities inside and out. What these men accomplished was an overflow of who they had become in their innermost beings as a consequence of an ongoing relationship that existed 24/7 between them and their God. As their beliefs were transformed and their worldviews revolutionized, they offered truth to multitudes of people who came under their influence.

God's disruptive methodology was at work—the insignificant birthing the significant, the unknown replacing the well known, a transformed life resulting in a disruptive lifestyle.

The first man was Joseph. A master of dreams, he was sold into slavery at a young age and ended up in a prison cell in Egypt. When Pharaoh had disturbing nightmares, this uneducated, lower-class Hebrew prisoner warned the Egyptians about an oncoming famine. Pharaoh ultimately made Joseph second-in-command, and Joseph eventually saved the nation of Israel from starvation—including his own family who he chose to forgive and save.

The second man was Moses, who, after committing murder, entered a self-imposed exile and lived an inconspicuous existence. He wanted to achieve great things for God in the spotlight but was thrown backstage for a season. Moses then settled down, got married, and became a shepherd. Then one day, he was confronted by the famous burning bush. Dramatic events took place in the desert where Moses led the Israelites. God used this exile not only to free His chosen people but to also demonstrate His power before Egypt and the surrounding nations. The one true God destroyed the fine-tuned Egyptian war machine. Moses' life was transformed, revealing the disruptive methodology of God.

The third man was Saul, who was transformed into the apostle Paul—murderer and martyr-maker turned missionary. Religious patriarch turned church planter. Agitator turned author. His life was turned inside out through God's disruption.

With all three men, their relational transformational journey was the cause, while their disruptive lifestyle was the effect.

They were not mere church members who secured their tickets to Heaven. They were not mere believers who behaved because of an obligatory reverence to their God. Rather, they were paradigm shifters, overcomers, culture crafters, and history makers. We must consider what it means to be changed forever to:

- Challenge the status quo
- Change the culture
- Champion a new trail

All the stories in the Bible involve this same life disruption principle. Noah, Abraham, David, Queen Esther, Rahab, Daniel, the Israelites, the disciples, Martha and Mary, the apostles, and the members of the early church are all examples of God's disruption of life.

God was not then—and is not today—in the business of simply changing behavior or issuing tickets to Heaven to those who believe. Challenging the status quo, changing culture, and championing a new trail were consequences of God's disruption of life in these people. There was an inter-dimensional inter-play between their spirit-mind-body that went beyond mere belief to an experiential reality of God *in* humanity.

God is about:

* Birthing an ongoing relationship between an individual and Himself on earth through spiritual rebirth of the human spirit. The re-birth of the human spirit is not a metaphor or a parable, but is literal
* Establishing an incredible interdimensional interplay between the dimension of God and the human spirit, cognitively recognized in the mind and expressed through the body. This differentiates biblical Christianity from the religion called Christianity as well as all other religions of the world
* Creating a new identity and enabling humanity to experience the identity called child of God—a Father and child relationship that we all long for in our inner being and resets us to who we were always meant to be, literally!
* Filling the cosmic vacuum so, whether in the heights of success or in the depths of failure and everywhere in between, there is an inner constant that fills and fulfills in the midst of external variables, literally!
* Transforming lives from the inside out so culture is changed, literally!
* Empowering people to become champions in the everyday realities of life, literally!

The message of this book centers around a pivotal question: What separates the Christian whose life has been changed from the child of God whose life changes the world?

The Ultimate Disruptor

The greatest disruption in history occurred when Jesus came to earth as both God and man—all of God inside a person. His very life was a disruption. His message was a disruption. His purpose was a disruption.

He came to replace:

+ The Old Covenant with the New Covenant
+ The old way of doing with a new way of being
+ The old creation with a new creation
+ The old law with a new life

Jesus was:

+ Born of a virgin in a barn among animals, the son of a carpenter, raised in a disrespected town, and the antithesis of all expectations for the Jewish Messiah and the Savior of humanity
+ The Creator who had no place to lay His head
+ The Deliverer who rode into Jerusalem not on a white horse but on a borrowed donkey
+ The Savior crucified between two thieves
+ The King born into insignificance

Jesus challenged the established system and, in so doing, launched a community-driven grass-roots movement that would consistently challenge the status quo and redefine the meaning of human life throughout history.

The cross—the ultimate symbol of death—became the definitive symbol of victory and purpose. The cross also became the birthplace of humanity's new identity by bringing us into a love relationship with God Himself. Jesus came to change our being through an ongoing love relationship with God Himself, transforming human nature so anyone who so chooses may possess and experience the life God offers (John 3:16–17).

The ultimate disruption of life happens when God takes residence in us, communing with us, relating to us, transforming us, and redefining human identity.

Jesus Christ is the *only* Person who:

+ Promises a personal and spiritual relationship with humanity, filling the inner emptiness resulting in transformational lifestyle
+ Shows the way of salvation, not as a series of events done by mankind but as a relational journey between God and mankind

+ Demonstrates that Heaven starts here on earth for mankind
+ Does not demand our performance but transforms us to be like Him so we can become like Him and therefore as a consequence behave like Him.

The cross of Christ is unique because it has transformational consequences *in* mankind. The fundamental difference between the religion of Christianity and the relationship that the cross births is what happens *after* belief. In religion, humanity awaits a future paradise as a consequence of belief, while desperately trying to meet present behavioral standards. In relationship, belief results in a new dimension re-birthed in humanity, experiencing a present transformation of the mind by the new spiritual dimension. This results in cognitively experiencing God in the present, which consequentially expresses itself externally, and Heaven is only a logical progression from one dimension to another.

The biblical gospel is good news because it can produce:

+ Spiritual rebirth in the present
+ Transformation of the mind so humanity can experience that spiritual rebirth by cognitively recognizing the embrace of the Father
+ A reset in the alignment of human nature with the divine nature, resulting in wholeness or holiness in humanity
+ Transformation of the mind, where we become people of love, peace, and unity

Crossruption is about encountering God, not as a belief, but as an experience that goes beyond emotion and intellect, resulting in a new creation. Human beings long for this experience of spiritual communion, which fills their inner emptiness. The mirage of life stops here. The cosmic vacuum is filled here.

BEING AND DOING

The cross births a Christian being, which results in Christian doing (actions).

The cross births Christ's being in mankind, which results in Christ's doing through mankind.

We can have Christian doing without Christ's being, but we can never have Christ's being without Christian doing.

So if there is no Christlike behavior, this is because Christ is not rebirthed in the person. Christianity is not about desperately trying to mimic Christlike behavior but being transformed into Christ's nature. If there is a problem with a mango tree bearing fruit, the gardener doesn't try to fix the fruit, he focuses on the tree.

Crossruption is not about introducing a new idea but about reviving and realigning with the same one the followers of Jesus experienced—the same one Joseph, Moses, and Paul faced, and the same one I finally came to grips with on my own journey.

This is not just another trendy faith fad that, once implemented, will make us all happy and healthy. This is about a transformation that compels us to leave our old lives and follow Jesus into His new life—not to go to work *for* Him in the same old boat with the same old nets, but to join Him *in* His work, a whole new way of fishing (Matthew 4:19).

Crossruption is a call to all those who recognize their inner emptiness, are haunted by the cosmic vacuum inside, and are ready to stop chasing after the mirage of life.

A Personal Journey

My dad was extremely committed to the local church, which was always a part of our family culture. He spent most of his Sundays at church and was a great father, as well as husband, in the foundational years of my life.

As a result of my dad's spiritual zeal, I was immersed in the church and the language of the Bible, and was continually surrounded by faith. I learned about Jesus, talked about Him, and even acted like Him. The church was my second home.

I was an asthmatic child who desperately wanted to have my own identity, but I couldn't find that in academics or sports. I felt I had no gifts, no special skills. The church became a place where I could excel. I learned to do Christianity by performing. I could gain satisfaction and the approval of others by behaving the way everyone else did. But acting out Christianity became more difficult when I was a teenager. I couldn't keep up this level of performance over the long term.

Unable to maintain the standard, I eventually tried to escape my feelings of emptiness through substance abuse. As a teenager, I would skip school, enjoy myself, and then feel miserable the next morning as I sobered up or went through withdrawal. I would then start the cycle all over again. By age seventeen, I had suffered liver damage. I was admitted to the hospital and couldn't take my twelfth-grade exams.

As I lay in a hospital room, my older brother visited me and asked a very difficult question: "If you died tonight, do you know where you would go?" Other than sharing the same birthday date, my brother and I had little in common. He was six years older and had his life together. He was healthy, had excelled in school, and had become a chemical engineer. And now he was asking me a question I couldn't answer that night or for many days to follow.

When I was well enough to go home, my brother gave me a Bible, and I began reading it. I accepted Christ and was as faithful as I could be to live the Christian life. To a large extent, I was successful. I went on to college, got married, and had two children. I worked at various businesses and was gradually healed of my physical problems, including the asthma that had plagued me for most of my childhood.

I succeeded in business. I succeeded in life. Outwardly, I was living the "American dream." Financially, socially, and supposedly spiritually, I could have asked for nothing more. Feeling totally secure in all areas of life, I believed in Jesus. I did great work on His behalf and lived out the perfect Christian story.

Or did I?

Inside I felt a void I could not explain. Though I was acting the right way, I could not escape the questions inside me.

Why were my spiritual achievements not bringing lasting fulfillment? After all, I was doing all the right things. I had realized my sin and had encountered God. Life was great, as He gave me health, wealth, and influence. What a deal for me! I had everything that people dream about, but inside something was still missing. I had the gifts of the Spirit and the "encounter with God" but still did not know the Person I was so enthusiastically working for and promoting.

As this inner emptiness and longing continued, I kept telling myself to believe—to believe God lived in me, to believe He loved me, to believe everything written in the Bible. But the more I believed and behaved, the more I felt the vacuum within.

God created each of us with a "me" inside. Call it consciousness or self-awareness or whatever you will, but human beings have no choice except to contend with the need to fill that "me" vacuum.

The residence of "me" is not physical or intellectual but spiritual. "Me" is where a person's identity is defined and experienced. The mind understands this, and the body expresses it.

My questions raged inside:

- Does Jesus live in me, or am I supposed to believe He lives in me?
- Am I supposed to believe God is my Father, or am I supposed to experience Him as my Father?
- Am I supposed to believe in His love and peace, or am I supposed to experience His love and peace?
- Were Jesus' stories only metaphors and parables, or were they truths I am called to experience?
- Am I to believe in having a relationship with Jesus, or do I have a relationship with Jesus?

Who I was on the inside and what others saw on the outside—my belief, my experience, and my expression—did not match up. As a result, I was a circumstantial Christian. Let me explain this term.

I lived out my identity based solely on external situations. On Sundays, I could express my faith at church. But on the weekdays, I depended on my circumstances. My Christianity was like a chameleon, and I was constantly adjusting my colors to blend in with my settings.

Who I was at church on Sunday was different from who I was with my family, which was different from who I was in my business relationships, which was different from who I was when I was alone. I had a rationale for this, but I knew inside that something was very wrong.

The Christianity I had come to practice consisted of behavior triggered by belief and intellect. This brand of Christianity had me at the center and allowed me to change my behavior based on my circumstances. I decided how and where to express my Christian identity and was told this was normal, for all that mattered was if I believed in Jesus.

The hypocrisy of my spiritual life, the duality of my faith experience, led me on a journey to know this God who calls Himself Father, this God who expressed Himself in the person of His Son Jesus Christ, this God who said He would live inside me in the person of the Holy Spirit. If the apostle Paul could say, "I want to know Him better," the same was also demanded of me.

This was a turning point in my life. I had reached a crossroads, a point of disruption. No—a *Crossruption*!

This was a season in my journey when I realized I could no longer outsource my faith or buy a product called God. Jesus had come to disrupt lives, and He was at this moment disrupting mine!

I had found it possible to do church and God without experiencing either. The spiritual activity that should have brought fulfillment did not. My business, financial, and Christian achievements could not fill the vacuum inside me. The emptiness and the brokenness sent me on a journey to know this God who had so profoundly affected my life.

How did I realize that I belonged to this religion called Christianity and was far away from the relationship that Jesus was calling me to? What did I do? Where did I go? How did I hit the reset button of my Christianity? In short, through the Bible. I tossed out all my religious, denominational, cultural, racial, and geographic filters. The only filter I kept was God's Word. With new eyes, I studied the Scripture. This led me on the journey I remain on to this day, communing with my God. He longs to do this with each one of us.

THE GREAT DISRUPTION

An intimate inner communion has allowed a rich spring of living water (John 4:10–11) to flow inside me, transforming me so that same water can flow through me. I would not trade this blessed communion for anything. I have a love relationship with Jesus, an inner Tent of Meeting (Exodus 27–40; 1 Corinthians 3:16) inside me through which I have access through the Holy Spirit. This is not a belief but a deep personal spiritual experience as a consequence of my belief. It has nothing to do with external circumstances or the countless external variables of life. This is not an emotional ride manipulated by music and ambience. This is not an intellectual puffing up of knowledge. Spirituality is not about emotionality, nor is it about intellectuality. The spirituality of the Bible took me beyond mind and body and set me firmly on a dimension that is the very home of God Himself, who is Spirit.

Irrespective of what happens on the outside, an inner love and peace remains anchored by the Father Himself. My mind, which comprehends the realm of the Spirit where my identity as a child of God is forged and experienced, cannot be compromised. In this communion of intimacy, inside this love relationship, my mind is transformed into the mind of Christ (1 Corinthians 2:16). My identity comes through the renewal of my mind (Romans 12:2). The Spirit of God takes the Word of God and transforms me into the image of Christ (2 Corinthians 3:18). Knowing and experiencing God is not a belief, but a personal experience as a consequence of belief.

What happens *to* me no longer matters, because what happens *in* me defines what happens *through* me. There is an inner fullness that comes from the spiritual dimension which is progressively experienced through the transformation of the mind. In fact, the satisfaction I derive from the things of the mind and body pale in comparison so I progressively gravitate towards living by the Spirit.

What I possess and what I achieve do not define me, but they are the greatest channels of enabling community development around the world. It is incredible to live a life not being defined by what we possess, what we achieve, and what others think of us, but to live a life defined by who we are as children of God, not as an intellectual belief but a transformational experience.

No one ever again needs to tell me to "take a stand for Jesus," for that is not what I do but it is who I become and am becoming more and more. Living for Jesus is no more the cause but an incredible effect that overflows. An internal freedom allows me to live my intended identity unreservedly on the outside—anywhere, everywhere, with anyone.

How could King David, one of the greatest leaders in history, a ruler who had more possessions, power, and privilege than most men could dream of, declare that he would rather spend time with God than be anywhere else

(Psalm 84:10)? God satisfied David in his spirit more than anything He gave him—not in what David did for God or in what God did through David.

How can this be? Can God be our chief end?

Is it possible:

+ To live a lifestyle of not only moral reformation but also spiritual transformation leading to communion, communication, and companionship with God?
+ To live a lifestyle of being whole internally with the ability to overcome self-destructive behaviors?
+ That the purpose of God for us is not our purpose for God?
+ That we could move from a purpose-driven life to a Person-driven life?
+ To move from finding our identity in our purpose to finding our identity in the Person of Christ?

The answer is a resounding yes!

How could Daniel, written about in the Old Testament, defy the law of the land and be willing to be thrown to the lions for the sake of his God? How could Daniel face the visible threats with this invisible God? Who was God to Daniel? What transformed this man so much that what happened to his life no longer mattered? How could Daniel think the way he did?

How was Stephen, written about in the New Testament, enabled to bless those who were stoning him to death? How could Stephen think to pray for the people who were killing him?

We must realize this truth today. When killing is done in the name of God, what is the biblical response? Love. However, love is not what we do but who we become. When we become love, love will flow from us. When we only imitate love, we love selectively and conditionally. Daniel, who had access to all the wealth of the kingdom, and Stephen, who was simply a common poor man, derived their identities from the same Source—not from their circumstances but from their God.

How could the early church be salt and light? How could Peter be shackled in prison and still be able to sleep in peace? Who is this God who calmed the storm and saved the boat when Jesus was there but destroyed the boat and saved Paul from drowning? How could Paul be the same man whether he was alone inside a prison or in front of Caesar? Why did neither circumstance or location define his identity? What was the secret to Paul's consistent expression of Christ's identity? How could the early church follow the law of God while also defying the law of the land? How could Peter and John say to the religious leaders, "Which is right in God's eyes: to listen to you, or to him?" (Acts 4:19)?

Men and women of God throughout history have experienced something far beyond believing, far beyond having the right theological knowledge. They underwent a total identity transformation beyond intellectual information. The people of God were not acting, faking, or imitating. Their thinking was transformed by and through the influence of another dimension. Because they thought differently, they behaved differently. They expressed their belief because of who they became. Something happened between their belief and their expression of belief.

Crossruption is all about how to experience that something—to bridge the gap between belief and expression to experience the belief before expression. The disciples' belief in Jesus gave birth to an inner realm of the Spirit, which they experienced through the renewal of their minds. And when they *experienced* Jesus, they became *like* Jesus and *expressed* Jesus. A personal inner experiential relationship with God results in an overflowing expression of God on the outside. What we all long for and what will satisfy our inner emptiness is not the right expressions but an experiential spiritual relationship with the Person of God.

Belief-based knowledge of God allows us to do brave things in the hope of an expected end. Experiential knowledge of God allows us to do brave things even when we cannot know the end.

I have named this lifestyle *Crossruption* because this term reflects the fact that Christ is the Great Disruptor, creating an internal transformation that is not about doing, producing, or going through the motions, but about experiencing God inside and then expressing Jesus to the culture.

The world's belief systems are about acknowledging, accepting, talking, and writing about, and promoting the experience. But *Crossruption* is about actually having the experience!

Let's say you want to spend a week in Hawaii. You acknowledge and accept that Hawaii is real, and you want to visit. You talk about it, read up on it, and tell anyone and everyone about the experience available there.

But when and how do you experience Hawaii? Only when you go there, put your feet in the sand, breathe the air, eat the food, and see the sights. You experience Hawaii only when you are in Hawaii.

At its core, this experience as a consequence of belief in Jesus involves:

- The rebirth of the human spirit and a new inner realm
- Transformation of the mind by the Spirit of God through the Word of God
- A transformational inner experience of intimacy with God
- A journey of the mind that becomes the mind of Christ
- A lifestyle of freedom having the ability to not do what we do not want to do
- An external expression of love and unity in community that goes beyond race, color, geography, and ethnicity
- An ongoing experience of the Spirit of God testifying with our spirits that we are children of God

Just like disruptive innovation, this transformation starts small but eventually encompasses everything. One day, there will be no trace of the old, for everything shall become new. And this is not a product or a service but your very life!

> Therefore, if anyone is in Christ, the new creation has come:
> The old has gone, the new is here! (2 Corinthians 5:17)

THE ART OF BEING

So you say that you:

- Have made a decision to follow Christ? Check.
- Have accepted Jesus? Check.
- Believe in Jesus? Check.
- Regularly attend a church? Check.
- Have read much of the Bible? Check.
- Live a holy life? Check.

- ✦ Regularly participate in ministry or volunteer at your church? Check.
- ✦ Give to ministry and missions? Check.

But you still sense there is something more? The power of the disruption of Jesus starts with the individual. If you are fed up with the religion that Christianity has become—or with any other belief system for that matter—I want to help you move to a dynamic relationship with God through Christ, just as I did. This is biblical Christianity.

If you have confused emotion or intellect with spirituality, I want to open the doors to an intimacy with God that goes beyond a Sunday high and the Monday reality.

If you are a Christian living a private life of sin and a public life of holiness, I pray this book brings you real transformation. You can learn how to live beyond the triggers of the body and mind to live from the spiritual dimension.

If you are a Christian who finds a purpose to life in what you do for God or in what God does through you, this book will help you know intimacy with Him.

If you are a Christian experiencing the intimacy of God, I pray these pages will take you into deeper waters.

If you are not a Christian and are seeking true spirituality, my hope is that this book will open new doors to experiencing the one true God.

In the pages ahead, I will take you through the four stages of the journey of *Crossruption*. I have written this book to be followed as a sequential journey.

1—Original Creation

What was our original design? What was our original form and function?

2—Fallen Creation

How did we become who we are? What happened to us? Where did the operating system go wrong? Where did the design fault occur?

3—NEW CREATION

Why Jesus? Why the cross? How do we experience God? How do we experience what we believe? How can we experience a son or daughter identity? How are we to live out the moral and social compass of Jesus? What are the measurements of the Christian faith?

We all know what to do, but doing is a consequence of who we become, so this section outlines how to bridge the gap between having the knowledge and experiencing the knowledge.

4—FUTURE CREATION

How is the present connected to the future? What happens to us after physical death?

Crossruption is about my journey. While I am still a pilgrim, I invite you to come with me. You will find no religion here. You will find no performance here, only a private journey of Spirit-to-spirit communion with God.

Jesus is the journey, and He becomes the destination. Your destination!

PART II
·ORIGINAL DESIGN

So God created mankind in his own image, in the image of God he created them; male and female he created them. God blessed them. (Genesis 1:27–28)

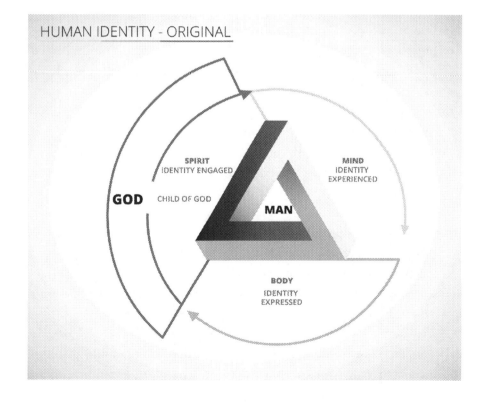

HUMAN IDENTITY - ORIGINAL

SPIRIT
IDENTITY ENGAGED

MIND
IDENTITY
EXPERIENCED

GOD CHILD OF GOD

MAN

BODY
IDENTITY
EXPRESSED

UNDERSTANDING THE SPIRITUAL DIMENSION

When everything I had achieved in my mind and body—personal accomplishments, resources, and successes—did not satisfy me, I turned to a different dimension. I had belief in God, knowledge of Him, and emotional spiritual experiences, but there was a gap between what I believed and practiced.

I realized the spiritual dimension in human beings was not meant simply to be believed or acknowledged but to become an experiential reality with humanity designed to live in awareness of God from within. I craved what was written in Scripture about the interaction between God and humanity, with mankind taking part in the divine nature.

Understanding the spiritual dimension is the first step and the most difficult one in an age when news feeds and social media constantly offer us reports that we believe without question. We base many of our beliefs on the experiences of others. But when it comes to spirituality, we are unwilling to believe based on anyone else's personal experience.

In our culture, belief based on someone else's evidence is acceptable, except when it comes to God and spirituality, and then we must always demand evidence first before belief. The fact remains that evidence will not always lead to belief, but belief will always lead to evidence in the areas of spirituality that the Bible reveals.

Life's best experiences always start with believing and hoping that something exists beyond what we see. The greatest inventions in history resulted from this mindset. In many areas of life, we believe without validation. For example, how many people have tested their parents' DNA against theirs to prove their own legitimacy? So I plead that you will give the benefit of the doubt to a dimension in each of us that is beyond mind and body—the spiritual dimension.

For me, the first step was to accept the realities of the spiritual dimension and all this might entail. To fill the cosmic vacuum inside me, I had to start by understanding that my identity is fundamentally spiritual. The answer to "Who am I?" had to go beyond the variables of my mind and body. To experience this inner constant I had to know how I was originally designed to function. I needed to understand the identity of God, His function and personality. I had to come to grips with the reality of an enemy mentioned throughout the Bible and understand his purpose.

As I examined all the theories about how we arrived on the planet, I looked closely at Intelligent Design. The amazing entrepreneurs of the world were designing disruptive solutions, so what if I was intended to be a disruptive design myself? What if we *all* were? What if the way we have been "assembled" was more than a bunch of molecules coming together? What if there was indeed another dimension beyond mind and body that humanity could experience without the hypocrisy of religion?

I realized that the way we are wired is fundamentally different from the rest of creation, and, hence, we have problems that are vastly different from those of all other species. Why are we the only creatures on the planet fighting over rights, borders, and even religions? It is incredible how belief or unbelief in God is the primary reason for the greatest acts of terror. While the rest of creation struggles for food and survival, we fight over skin color or a place of worship.

We have an inner thirst for something more because we perceive the dimension of God Himself, who is Spirit! This is where human identity is found and defined. My goal in this section is to guide you from unbelief to belief in the spiritual realm, as well as to provide knowledge of this realm, allowing you to experience this amazing dimension beyond mind and body in the subsequent sections.

Expressing belief, gaining knowledge, speaking, singing, and writing about God are one thing. To experience the Spirit of God intertwining with our minds in a relationship of love is something entirely different. If we are conscious of the mind and body, we can be conscious of the dimension that defines human identity—that of the spirit—the way we have been designed to operate. That is home. That is rest. This is what we all long for. When all of life flows from this dimension, our intellectual and material pursuits take on a totally new meaning and purpose.

If I kept trying to solve the problem of my spirit within the realm of my mind, I would continue to struggle with complicated theological and philosophical questions. If I tried to satisfy the desires of my body and avoid my spirit, I would stay in this vicious cycle of emotional and intellectual highs and lows.

The concept of the supernatural is not unique to Christianity. Hinduism,

Islam, Buddhism, and most other religions are all about the supernatural. With the exception of those who do not believe in a god, everyone recognizes the supernatural dimension. But it is most often restricted to a place "way out there," to the super-religious, to the super-spiritual, or to simple belief. We cannot wrap our minds around a dimension beyond our intellect, and that is the root problem I will address. The key differentiator of the cross of Christ is its ability to interweave and integrate the three dimensions of mankind—spirit, mind, and body. The uniqueness of Christianity is the experiential integrating reality of God in mankind—Immanuel, which means "God with us." The reality of the Vine and the branch which is intimately inter-connected with inter-communication and communion at a level that goes beyond belief. The reality of the body of a man or woman becoming the Temple of God where the residence of God is not a belief, which is idolatry, but becomes a literal reality.

The Identity Challenge: The "I" of Mankind

India is home to some of the most delicious mangoes in the world. But over the last half century of my experience with this fruit, it has been disappointing to see how the taste and quality have changed. I still remember the taste of this fruit in the 1970s, and for me, today's mangoes are like counterfeits. However, for my children, who have not tasted what I have, these counterfeits are the originals! Through experience, I know the difference; they do not and cannot.

Banks do not train workers to find counterfeit currency notes by showing them countless variations of copies but by making certain employees become very familiar with the originals. When tellers know the real thing, they can quickly spot the fakes.

We have all experienced the originals in many areas of life. We also have experienced the counterfeits. We have all longed for the original when only a copy was available. If we do not know the original, the counterfeit could easily become the real thing to us.

The longing inside all of us proves there is something more than what we experience now. We live in a counterfeit world but were created to experience the original. We are surrounded by artificiality, from the "sugar" in our coffee to the "leather" shoes we wear to the "diamonds" in our jewelry to our "friends" on social media. In all this, we have a deep sense that there is something more to life. We feel a void that we can't seem to fill permanently.

The evidence for historical truth is the experience of present reality. The evidence for God creating humanity is not a belief system but our experience of inner emptiness. If there is one area where historical truth is evidenced by present experience, it is spirituality.

The *Crossruption* journey begins with understanding our identity in the original design. Knowing who we were meant to be is the first step to experiencing who we can become. The topics covered in this section might seem somewhat abstract at times, but this discussion is critical to advancing to specifics later on in this book. Knowing theoretical concepts helps us experience practical value. Knowing the laws of nature enables scientists to discover and innovate. Therefore, it is worth the effort to understand so we can experience abundant life!

The *Oxford Dictionary* defines *identity* as "the fact of being who or what a person or thing is." Thus identity is not an action, attribute, or even a character.

> Then God said, "Let the land produce vegetation: seed-bearing plants and trees on the land that bear fruit with seed in it, according to their various kinds." (Genesis 1:11)

> And God said, "Let the land produce living creatures according to their kinds: the livestock, the creatures that move along the ground, and the wild animals, each according to its kind." (Genesis 1:24)

The simplest way to understand the fact of being, or human identity, is to understand the Hebrew word *miyn* for "kind." God created vegetation, animals, and birds "each according to its kind." So, each creation of God had its own *miyn*, which defined its unique characteristics. The essence of an animal or a plant comes from its being or identity. The *miyn* of all living creation—other than humans—is defined in the genetic makeup.

Pretend for a moment that a plant could talk. You ask the plant, "What are you?" It answers, "I am a plant." But if you ask, "Why are you a plant?" it would not say, "Because I have roots" or "Because I bear seeds." It would say, "I am a plant because that is what I am."

For the sake of educational understanding, science teaches us identity through characteristics, but a plant is a plant because of its intrinsic *miyn*. Do you see how we have been taught to identify everything by what it *does* and what it *has*, not by what it *is*? And also how we define human identity only by characteristics like color, race, religion, and geography? While actions and attributes express identity, they do not define it. In all of creation, actions and attributes are programmed in the DNA.

While attributes are programmed into the DNA of human beings, the identity of human beings is not. When a plant is uprooted and destroyed, its DNA is destroyed; its identity is destroyed. Everything is gone. Human identity is not and should not be defined by attributes and characteristics. Possessing amazing beauty and unique design, it is defined only in the incredible spiritual dimension that we all long to experience.

Physical destruction of creation brings its existence to a close. Human beings are the exception. There is something left after the destruction of the body and mind of mankind, and that "something" is where the identity of mankind is defined and experienced.

THE 3-D IDENTITY OF HUMAN BEINGS

God made human beings with a 3-D identity.

> Then God said, "Let us make mankind in our image, in our likeness." (Genesis 1:26)

This is one of the most incredible statements in the Bible. God did not speak humanity into existence as He did all the rest of His creation. Pay close attention to these four key statements:

- Nothing else has as its *miyn* the image or likeness of God.
- Human beings are different, for we have the *miyn of* God.
- Human beings have a different identity because we have a different method of creation.
- No other creation enjoys the creation-Creator connection that we do.

When you combine the nature of God, which is Spirit, with the reflection and image of God in humanity, it is obvious that human beings were created with a spiritual dimension. If the mind and body are true, then the human spirit is equally true. The connection between God and humanity is the spirit in human beings.

God created human beings as a 3-D creation with a spirit that communes and communicates with God, a mind—an emotional and intellectual conscious and subconscious component that understands and comprehends God—and a physical body that expresses God from the internal to the external.

Plant DNA differs from animal DNA, and the main difference is found in the physiological and physical realms. The difference between human beings and all other creation is not just physiological and physical. The game-changer in humans—the disruptor—is a different dimensional attribute. We were created with three faculties—body, mind, and spirit. We experience our identity in the spirit; we understand that identity in the mind and express it through the body.

A fish swims in water because it is a fish. A fish isn't a fish because it swims. Swimming isn't what identifies a fish, because not everything that swims is a fish. The identity of a fish goes beyond this primary attribute of the species. A fish is a fish because of what it is—*miyn*.

Human beings have the ability to ask these questions:

+ Who am I?
+ Where did I come from?
+ What am I doing here?
+ Where am I going?

The human mind cannot be satisfied with this uncertain state. There are many questions that remain unanswered in the human mind, but the biggest one is regarding personal identity. This question is what puts us in this cyclical race to find the meaning of life. In fact, philosophy is the best evidence of humanity's 3-D nature. The debate over the existence of God, which entails the search for something more, reflects this.

Though spirit, mind, and body are interdependent, the spirit is unique.

The mind and body can die, but the spirit never will. God created the human spirit to be immortal. This spirit defines the human identity.

The realm of the spirit is not consciousness, sub-consciousness, imagination, intelligence, or even thinking. The spirit can influence the mind, which then influences every aspect of the body.

Today, everything related to the human brain is programmable and replicable. Imagine a day when the brain is replicated in "the cloud" and is able to exist outside time and space. When this occurs, and it is likely only a matter of time as science progresses, human immortality would be accomplished. But the person who created the immortal consciousness in the cloud would still die longing for meaning and purpose in life. The "person" that was created would continue to exist as mountains and valleys have existed from time immemorial, with self-evident purpose and meaning. Anything born other than through the union of a woman's egg and a man's sperm is an "it" that does not carry the third human dimension—the spirit. The inventor would therefore have created an extremely intelligent human-like "it."

So, is there objective evidence of the spirit dimension, something beyond theoretical belief? The answer is an absolute yes. In fact, that is the game-changer in Christianity, but like the mangoes of the '70s, we have moved so far away from the normal that the present normal looks abnormal! We predominantly have a spiritual counterfeit that has become the new original.

> For those who are led by the Spirit of God are the children of God. (Romans 8:14)

But how can we be "led" if we do not know how to recognize the Person leading? The Scriptures do not tell us simply to believe in being "led by the Spirit of God" but declare that those led through an experiential reality are the children of God. Our identity as such is proven in knowing and being led by His Spirit. This is who we were, and this is who we can become once again. Experiential knowledge of the truth sets us free from the counterfeit.

FUNCTIONALITY OF THE SPIRIT DIMENSION IN MANKIND

We must better understand the role of the Spirit in the original design and how we can have communion, communication, and companionship with God. The relationship between God and Adam and Eve took place in the realm of the spirit. As people living in the realm of the mind and body, we find it incomprehensible that in the original design human beings lived through another dimension.

In their original state, human beings reflected God. Though God and humans were independent beings, humans experienced their identity through their relationship with Him. The Spirit of God communed with the spirit of Adam, while Adam's spirit communed with his mind and his mind communed with his body. Humans functioned inter-dimensionally. Just as we experience the interplay now between the mind and body, the original was designed to interplay between spirit, mind, and body.

Science may be able to offer an alternate body and mind, but the spiritual dimension cannot be programmed. When human advancement finally encodes itself into machines, they will be extremely intelligent. The men and women who create those machines will die physically but will live spiritually for eternity, but the machines will die when the energy supply is depleted.

Human beings cannot commune with fire, air, or water because there is a dimension difference. Humans are designed to have a relationship with God through Spirit-to-spirit communion, to experience communion in the mind and express that communion through the body.

COMMUNION AND COMMUNICATION IN COMMUNITY

> When the woman saw that the fruit of the tree was good for food and pleasing to the eye, and also desirable for gaining wisdom, she took some and ate it. She also gave some to her husband, who was with her, and he ate it. Then the eyes of both of them were opened, and they realized they were naked; so they sewed fig leaves together and made coverings for themselves. (Genesis 3:6–7)

Prior to eating the fruit, the woman saw through the realm of the spirit. But when Adam and Eve ate the fruit, their eyes were opened in the physical realm and closed to the spiritual. The way Adam and Eve "saw" in verse 6 is different from the way they "saw" in verse 7. This is consistent in many places throughout the Bible where we read about people being given "eyes to see" in the spiritual realm.

> When the servant of the man of God got up and went out early the next morning, an army with horses and chariots had surrounded the city. "Oh no, my lord! What shall we do?" the servant asked. "Don't be afraid," the prophet answered. "Those who are with us are more than those who are with them." And Elisha prayed, "Open his eyes, Lord, so that he may see." Then the Lord opened the servant's eyes, and he looked and saw the hills full of horses and chariots of fire all around Elisha. (2 Kings 6:15–17)

In verse 15, Elisha's servant sees with his physical eyes. In verse 17, the Lord opens his spiritual eyes so he can see through his physical eyes. The servant sees the realm of the invisible, which becomes as real to him at that moment as the realm of the visible.

> Philip found Nathanael and told him, "We have found the one Moses wrote about in the Law, and about whom the prophets also wrote—Jesus of Nazareth, the son of Joseph." "Nazareth! Can anything good come from there?" Nathanael asked. "Come and see," said Philip. When Jesus saw Nathanael approaching, he said of him, "Here truly is an Israelite in whom there is no deceit." "How do you know me?" Nathanael asked. Jesus answered, "I saw you while you were still under the fig tree before Philip called you." Then Nathanael declared, "Rabbi, you are the Son of God; you are the king of Israel." (John 1:45–49)

In verse 48, Jesus tells Nathanael He saw him before Philip called him. Jesus had visual capability through the dimension of the spirit. All the book of Revelation is written in the dimension of the spirit as revealed to John. So the realm of the spirit is not mystical, spooky, or emotional but a dimension with full functionality that began with the creation of mankind. Living in and through the supernatural is normal operating procedure and not the glamorous, celebrity-driven, emotional culture the religion of Christianity predominantly portrays today.

The spiritual and physical dimension in humans has been designed for inter-dimensional communion and communication, for that is where humanity experiences the companionship of God Himself. We have been designed to experience a natural connection with the supernatural.

THE ROLE OF THE MIND

> The Lord God took the man and put him in the Garden of Eden to work it and take care of it. … Now the Lord God had formed out of the ground all the wild animals and all the birds in the sky. He brought them to the man to see what he would name them; and whatever the man called each living creature, that was its name. So the man gave names to all the livestock, the birds in the sky and all the wild animals. (Genesis 2:15, 19–20)

The brain—the human mind—is one of the most incredibly designed parts of the human body. While its creativity and intelligence are without peer, the human mind was not designed to exist and operate on its own. Just as the mind needed a body to express itself, the mind was designed to be in connection with the human spirit, which was in perfect connection, communion, communication, and companionship with another Source. The human mind was designed to be the connector between the spirit and the body. The mind and body on their own, without a relational spiritual communion with God, was not part of the original human design.

The mind was intended to use only one source to define its identity. If the original design had not been corrupted, we would have created beautiful civilizations, amazing products and technology, and incredible entertainment, all living in love, contentment, and peace.

The human mind was designed to find meaning and purpose in relational communion with God, not in what it did or in what it achieved. Our identity of who we are—the answer to the question "Who am I?"—is defined in the spirit of human beings, experienced in the human mind, and expressed through the human body.

When the mind cognitively experiences its identity from the spirit, it does not need to derive its identity from the intellectual, physical, or external activities. Security of who we are (identity) is a fundamental need that the human mind needs to experience. This is how we were designed, and there is no escape. This security of who we are is derived from the spirit and cognitively experienced in the mind, and the consequence is a human being who is complete in self-esteem and self-worth. The achievements of the mind and body can never bring lasting value to the human mind.

The mind could never survive with just the body. From day one, it also required an identity. The inner vacuum we feel is the evidence of a mind without an identity, a mind without a relation of spiritual communion, a mind longing for a foundation, a place where it was and where it is supposed to be. This cosmic vacuum points to the reality of the original design. There is a neighborhood between our ears which hears noises and voices that can be silenced by the Spirit of God.

While the mind of mankind and the mind of God have always been independent, they were once in perfect harmony. Spirit-to-spirit communication was standard in the original creation, and the mind was capable of recognition, comprehension, interpretation, and execution.

The mind did not control the spirit; the spirit controlled the mind, which was under the umbrella of the Spirit of God. The human spirit was in perfect union with its Designer. Spirit, mind, and body were interconnected and synchronous. The human mind communed with God and comprehended its identity. In this, there was an amazing recognition of God. Love was not emotional. The human spirit was united in a communion of love with the Spirit of God, which was experienced by the mind and expressed through the body. Faith was not needed because there was nothing to hope for, and the unseen was seen. Adam and Eve did not simply believe in God's existence; they experienced Him in reality.

BIRTHRIGHT IDENTITY—PERSONAL IDENTITY

Human beings were created with their personal identity known in being children of God. This was the creational birthright of Adam and Eve. The intertwining of God in mankind in the spirit forged this identity. Human language fails to express the intimacy they had as Father and children in this love relationship. Throughout history, human beings have yearned for this intimacy and have expressed their longing through poetry and art, but Adam and Eve experienced this ultimate relationship, the very spiritual experience we desire, with every fiber of our beings today.

Adam was aware of his creation identity. Had you asked him, "Who are you?" he would not have answered, "I am a farmer." He would have declared, "I am a child of God." If you had asked, "What do you do?" he likely would have answered, "Farming is my work." Adam differentiated his personal identity from what he did.

Under the original design, Adam could live seamlessly out of his identity as a child of God. Nothing that Adam did defined who he was; he was defined only by his love relationship and by his position before God. His actions were simply an expression of his identity as a child of God. Adam had nothing to do with establishing the relationship that defined his identity but experienced it as a consequence of a Spirit-to-spirit communion.

An apple will remain an apple whether it is found on a tree, in a national chain store, or in a local farmers' market. An apple cannot transform itself into an orange based on circumstances because an apple derives its identity from a constant. External variables do not define the internal constant. So it was with Adam and Eve. Their personal identity defined who they were, and what they did expressed their status as children of God.

PRIVILEGE IDENTITY

> God blessed them and said to them, "Be fruitful and increase in number; fill the earth and subdue it. Rule over the fish in the sea and the birds in the sky and over every living creature that moves on the ground." (Genesis 1:28)

The personal identity that God gives to human beings carries blessings and privileges. The *position* of being sons and daughters results in the *privileges* of being sons and daughters. Position is the cause, while privilege is the effect. Position is identity, while privilege is the expression of that identity.

The privileges of being fruitful, living in increase, and filling, subduing, and dominating the earth intellectually and physically, all resulted from Adam and Eve's position as children of God. This did not define their personal identity.

If Adam and Eve had continued to live in the garden, they would have built the most lucrative corporations, developed an extravagant creative arts culture, and given birth to awesome scientists, mathematicians, and geniuses in every other human endeavor. Unlike today's prodigies, they would not have self-destructed through poor decisions or committed suicide after having achieved great things. They would not have killed people, because they were different from them.

Why? Because Adam and Eve's privileges did not define their self-worth, self-esteem, and personal identity but their position as children of God satisfied them totally, and they knew their accomplishments resulted from that status. All they did and achieved was an overflow of who they were in their relational communion with God. Their inner experience defined their external expression.

The incredible inner spiritual communion between God and humanity puts to rest our every need that our lack of self-worth constantly demands through our minds and bodies. The spiritual can perfectly satisfy the physical as the spiritual gives perfect meaning to the physical.

How incredible to live life *experiencing* identity and not striving to *gain* identity!

CORPORATE IDENTITY

God, Adam, and Eve had a perfect relationship. The two children, destined to multiply and rule the earth, lived in harmony. Their love relationship with the Father allowed them to flourish, and this defined the corporate identity.

Human beings were not meant to live as islands but in community.

They were created to recognize God, have a love relationship with Him, and live in love relationships with others.

If human beings had not been disconnected from the Source, they would have continued to draw their personal identity from God. The community that would have filled the earth would have had one primary identity—children of God. People would have recognized themselves for who they were—God's sons and daughters. The common thread knitting the communities of the world together would have been their relationship to their Creator—God the Father and His children filling the earth with His glory. Personal identity defined corporate identity in the original creation. "Who I am" defined community relationships. "What I do" was never a basis for defining relationships. Human relationships were based on inner constants not on external or emotional variables in the original design of God.

Diversity reigned with nothing creating divisions of hierarchy or status. Differences were not dividers, because man and woman were bound together as children of God and saw their differences through this unifying lens. This singular identity was intended to be the foundation of human relationship.

Whether their color was brown, black, yellow, or white did not matter, because their personal identity came not from their appearance but from their relationship to God. Common identity, not even language, was the basis for relationships.

Geographic location would not have been a factor in determining identity either. Regardless of where people lived, the common denominator was God—the preeminent Person in all relationships. Community was based solely on people's status as children of God. Nothing else mattered.

In the original design, if a man from England met a man from China, their relationship would not be based on their homeland but on their common identity as children of God. This commonality defined human relationships. People could celebrate *diversity* because they were united in *identity*. Unity of identity in the realm of the spirit ensures we do not have disunity because of the realm of the mind and body.

Those who claim to have their citizenship in Heaven cannot live defining their lives through divisions of color, race, religion, and denomination. This is such a contradiction to claim a common citizenship in Heaven and live a divisive and conflicting life here on earth.

Unique Identity

> The Lord God said, "It is not good for the man to be alone.
> I will make a helper suitable for him." ... But for Adam no
> suitable helper was found. (Genesis 2:18, 20)

These verses use the Hebrew phrase *ezer neged*—meaning "suitable." Nothing in all of creation was *ezer neged* for Adam. If Adam needed only a helper or a buddy, God could have created another man. But Adam didn't need another pair of hands to work the fields. If that were the case, God could have duplicated Adam over and over, building an army. Adam needed *neged*. Suitability was not an option but a unique design. Just as God and man were perfect, man and woman, as well as God and woman, would be suitable. Try running a car with a gasoline engine on diesel fuel to understand the suitability concept.

Creation of woman was not a matter of functionality but a creative design of suitability. Adam didn't just need a womb to bear babies, because procreation was not the primary purpose of the woman.

Neged translates roughly as "reflection; in front of; in the presence of." The rest of creation could not become *neged* for Adam, for it could not become one in the flesh with him or be his reflection. God made the woman from the man so the woman would be of the man and the two could become one, reflecting one another and reflecting God. A creational polarity difference between man and woman would make them come together in one flesh, rendering them suitable for one another. The apostle Paul puts it this way: "Husbands, love your wives, just as Christ loved the church and gave himself up for her. ... For this reason a man will leave his father and mother and be united to his wife, and the two will become one flesh. This is a profound mystery—but I am talking about Christ and the church" (Ephesians 5:25, 31–32).

The creation of woman involved far more than her flesh and her role—how she looked and what she would do. The suitability of the relationship between Adam and Eve was of far greater significance than the flesh of two people coming together to fulfill roles. When two men or two women come together to attempt the one-flesh relationship, they are challenging a fundamental human design.

A man/man, woman/woman, man/animal, man/machine, or woman/plant relationship might fulfill the roles of the body and the mind at some level, but natural and human suitability will never be fully experienced. The fact that we have made homo- and heterosexual marriage a matter of fulfilling roles is fundamentally self-centered. Heterosexual marriage is no different from homosexual marriage if the *only* objective of the coming together is to fulfill a physical need and raise a family. The uniqueness of a man and woman coming together goes beyond the tendencies of the mind and body to solely fulfill roles. Humanity could come up with any number of human relationships; as long as we do not experience supernatural love inside, we will never be able to love one another for who we are. Hetero- or homosexual relationships would not satisfy humanity, for in both these relationships, we long for something more! We desperately try to replace emotional love for spiritual love and keep going in circles, trying to find "true" love.

Adam and Eve loved one another for who they were and not for what they could benefit from one another. This is the perfect reflection of God in the human relationship. God loves man and woman for who they are and not for what they do for Him. The present evidence for this historical reality is our inner longing for this love relationship, of wanting to have someone who would love us for who we are and not for what we do or give. The number of songs written and the number of movies made where this perfect love relationship is portrayed reflects this inner longing irrespective of cultures and geographies. This is a unique identity of humanity.

The Identity of Wholeness

Living in perfect communion, communication, and companionship with God, made Adam and Eve complete. Their holiness was not about the absence of wrong actions but the perfecting completeness that humanity experienced in relationship with God. In the original design, holiness was a state of humanity, not a consequence of doing the right actions.

Adam and Eve operated from a state of holiness; therefore all they did was holy. This sequence is very important. Behavior didn't make them whole. Because they were perfect, their acts and actions were perfect.

Every act of "holiness" that we attempt today in the religions of the world is only evidence of the human spirit trying to seek the original wholeness of communion, communication, and companionship with the supernatural. We try to achieve this through external moral rehabilitation because we long for the inner restoration of the perfect relationship. Religion desperately tries to fix this design fault through moral and behavioral rehabilitation.

The Purpose in the Original Design

Adam's relationship with his loving Father gave meaning and purpose to his life. Adam did not and could not have done anything more to find meaning. His created position of being in communion, communication, and companionship with God was enough. Adam was made so he could delight in God and God in him.

All the creative work that Adam did was a reflection of the One who gave him life. Adam did not subdue the earth to find meaning and purpose in life because he already had it. The purpose of all other creation is experienced in their actions, but the purpose of mankind is experienced in the relationship with a Person.

Purpose and meaning to life is a cognitive state of experiential inter-dimensional relationship, a relational experience of an ongoing spiritual love relationship and not an ecstatic experience of temporary intellectual and physical achievement. The cross of Christ makes this relationship available so humanity may experience true meaning and purpose in life.

If we had asked Adam, "What gives you purpose in life?" he would not have pointed to all of his accomplishments and said, "This is what drives me and why I wake up every morning." Adam would have said, "My Father alone is the meaning and purpose of my life. My identity as His child fulfills my life. Purpose does not drive me. The Person drives me."

We long to say this and live in such a state of being. And we can! This is what *Crossruption* is all about.

Being children of God does not involve an ideology or an intellectual theology but a biography. There is a world of difference between seeking God for His purposes and seeking the God of purpose. Experiencing God is the meaning of life. Adam and Eve did not achieve a purpose; they experienced it. They did not discover the meaning of life; they experienced it in communion, communication, and companionship with God.

THE IDENTITY OF DEATH

In the present dimension in which we live, we understand death as an event that ends life. Plants, animals, and human beings all die, with death bringing life to a close. But when it comes to humanity, this is only partially true. There is another dimension in mankind beyond the mind and body that never dies. "So God created mankind in his own image, in the image of God he created them; male and female he created them" (Genesis 1:27). The image of God in human beings makes them immortal. The longing to live forever is unique to human beings, who exist with a spiritual realm created for eternity. Humanity was created *with* life and *for* life, not death.

The spirit is the only part of the composition of mankind that cannot die. The character of the spirit is immortality. Imagine a world where death does not exist and space was not a problem because the matter that constituted human beings was like air: unlimited.

Compare this with the world in which we live now where fear of death haunts humanity and imagine how our lifestyles would change if we knew death did not exist. We can live that lifestyle now. The fear of death did not exist in the original design and was never intended to be part of our vocabulary or our emotions. No realm of humanity was ever meant to die.

> He has made everything beautiful in its time. He has also
> set eternity in the human heart; yet no one can fathom what
> God has done from beginning to end. (Ecclesiastes 3:11)

Death had no place in God's purpose for mankind. If he had not decided to make a choice that contradicted God's instruction, we would not need cemeteries, funeral homes, or hearses.

To comprehend *Crossruption*, we must recognize that death was not part of the original design and God's intent for humanity was and still is immortality.

THE IDENTITY OF GOD

My journey from belief to knowledge to experience was fundamentally influenced by comprehending the personal identity of God. Everyone who believes in God has a perception and a definition of Him.

I realized that God has an identity outside His attributes. He is not God because of what He does but because of who He is. He is a personal God. Self-existence—having no creator—is not an attribute of God. That is who He is. Had He not created the world and human beings with which to interact, He would be no less God. Even if God does nothing other than be who He is, He does not lose His identity.

The being or the identity of God is constant. By His very nature, He is God. There cannot be more or less God. All His actions, attributes, and manifestations come from His nature. Therefore, God is God, not because we have agreed He exists. His existence is not contingent upon human thinking. God is God because of His identity of self-existence.

The reality of time and space makes it difficult to understand self-existence. There was no starting point for time. God is in the dimension of the ever-present, and humanity is in the dimension of time and space. An amazing eternal dimension looks into yesterday, today, tomorrow, and on to eternity. Humanity on the other side restricted by time and space gazes into the dimension where there is no time and space to try and comprehend timelessness. The revelation of this truth is so universal for it is reflected in everything from the movies we watch to the scriptures of various religions. God from eternity to eternity is inseparable and a totally integrated Being.

The glory of God is not the same as the God of all glory, but they are intrinsically intertwined. In the original design, human beings had the awesome privilege of beholding God as He is without separating His Person from His attributes. The love and peace of God is not the same as the God of love and peace, but they are intrinsically intertwined.

All creatures lose who they are when their physical structure, character, attributes, and actions are removed. But God does not disappear when people declare He is dead. Human beings do not disappear when they die. God and humans do not need to do anything to define their identities because their identities have definitions beyond DNA. We often search for

God or try to prove His existence based on what we can prove He does. In the original design, mankind could not separate the being of God from the doing of God. He is one integrated Being of doing.

Here's a comparison. If we dismantle a car, we have parts of the car but no longer have the car. When we break down a vehicle to its parts, it loses its identity because its function is gone. An engine has no value sitting on blocks. A bucket seat has little value outside the interior of the vehicle. But when we put all the parts together, they become a car. Therefore, cars can gain and lose identity. As much as we want to take God apart, He is not built like anything we can comprehend. He is a total Being.

This Person of God is intertwined with His expression. Therefore, God can think, feel, get angry, know, see, plan, strategize, innovate, and disrupt. The realms of God are inextricable and intrinsically intertwined. There is absolutely no compartmentalization in Him. He is seamless, perfect, full, and complete.

The Bible describes God as a Person. We have almost lost this perspective because so many of us think of Him as a good ideology. We have relegated Him to a misty haze somewhere up in the skies or portrayed Him as a mystical tyrant waiting to whip us for our mistakes. God today is more often considered a thought or a figment of the imagination than a person! Our perception of God matters because it will define our relationship with Him.

> Moses said to God, "Suppose I go to the Israelites and say to them, 'The God of your fathers has sent me to you,' and they ask me, 'What is his name?' Then what shall I tell them?" God said to Moses, "I am who I am. This is what you are to say to the Israelites: 'I am has sent me to you.'"
> (Exodus 3:13–14)

Here we see God identifying Himself to Moses as the "I am who I am"—*Eheyeh asher Eheyeh*—the self-existent One, the eternal One. God is in effect telling Moses, "I am more than my name. My name is only an expression of who I am. Who I am is greater than what my name describes. My identity is not in my name or my actions."

IDENTITY

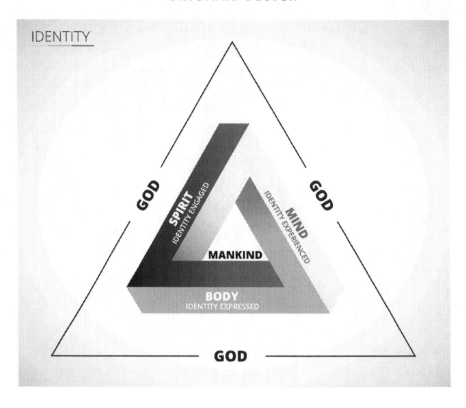

So who is God? He is the eternal self-existent One. He is the Alpha and the Omega (Revelation 1:8). God is not saying that He knows the beginning and the end but that He *is* the beginning and the end. This Great I Am is calling us to connect to Him, to this communion of relationship that humanity so desperately seeks and longs for. The communion, communication, and companionship that this book outlines for humanity to experience are with this incredibly awesome and amazing I Am, who has no beginning or end!

The Hebrew word for *father* is *Abba*. The Great I Am is Abba, or Father. The self-existent One is Abba. This is the starting point for experiencing God. If we wish to know the I Am, we must begin by understanding God's identity as the Father. We can know our own identity only by first knowing the fatherhood identity of God.

The Father identity of God is not the same as the universal fatherhood of God, with all human beings considered children of God because He is their Creator.

The fatherhood of God is a positional identity. God as Abba Father is a reality. God does not act like a father; He is our Father. Just as He is the self-existent One, the eternal One, He is our Father. Such is His identity. The starting point for biblical Christianity is the identity of God as our Father.

At the age of twelve, Jesus identified God as His Father: "Why were you searching for me?" he asked. "Didn't you know I had to be in my Father's house?" (Luke 2:49)

The Father identified the Son, and the identity of Jesus was revealed and sealed for all time. In this verse we see the Father's love expressed: "And a voice came from heaven: 'You are my Son, whom I love; with you I am well pleased'" (Mark 1:11).

Every other revelation of Jesus showing God as the Father flows from the fundamental identity of Jesus as the Son. This relationship would reflect the communion between the Father and the Son throughout Jesus' life on earth.

The Bible and Christianity carry no meaning apart from the understanding of God as Father. We must understand that God is relational and community is vital. He is seeking a spiritual relationship with us, a love relationship that happens through a communion of intimacy between a Father and child.

THE STRUCTURE OF GOD

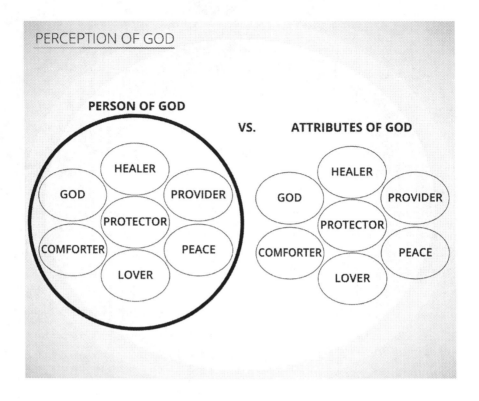

PERCEPTION OF GOD

As humans, we are conditioned by and familiar with structure from tiny atoms to vast galaxies. We know plants, animals, and our environment in microscopic detail. We can deconstruct all the things around us, determine their molecular patterns, and create synthetic replicas. We know the structure of oxygen, so we can produce artificial air and take it to places where there is none.

God is spirit, living and operating in another realm, another dimension. God is not the only being in that realm, though He is supreme. Angels reside there, as do Satan and his demons (fallen angels). "One day the angels came to present themselves before the Lord, and Satan also came with them" (Job 1:6).

In John 4:24 Jesus said, "God is Spirit." Oh, that we would comprehend this truth in the twenty-first century! We live in a time when only the tangible, visible, programmable, and comprehensible are regarded as truth. The spirit component is where the identity of God and mankind are defined and experienced. The spirit component is mankind's original code—the software, while the mind and body are the hardware. The expressions of God and His attributes do not define His identity as much as the expressions and attributes of mankind do not define identity. Performance is not the structure of God. Actions and attributes are not the structure of God.

Before we discovered how to analyze and produce air, we did not say it did not exist. We could sense air and be aware of it. The same is true with the spiritual realm. We cannot discount something just because we cannot understand it, or declare it to not exist just because we cannot see it, just because we can sense it but cannot touch it. We cannot see gravity either, but we experience it. The same concept applies to the spiritual realm.

By the end of this book, I hope and pray that you will understand and experience God just as you understand and experience air and gravity! As much as we experience these invisible elements naturally, we can experience the invisible God.

THE RELATIONAL IDENTITY OF GOD

God has a relational identity in that He relates intrinsically in the Trinity—the community made up of Father, Son, and Holy Spirit—and extrinsically as the Father of humanity. In both settings, we see God is a relational being.

> Then God said, "*Let us* make mankind in our image, in our likeness, so that they may rule over the fish in the sea and the birds in the sky, over the livestock and all the wild animals, and over all the creatures that move along the ground." (Genesis 1:26)

> In the beginning was the Word, and the Word was with God, and the Word was God. He was with God in the beginning. Through him all things were made; without him nothing was made that has been made. (John 1:1–3)

> "All this I have spoken while still with you. But the Advocate, the Holy Spirit, whom the Father will send in

my name, will teach you all things and will remind you of everything I have said to you." (John 14:25–26)

The human mind can only partially understand the intrinsic relationship in the Trinity. We human beings are so transactional in our current form that we cannot comprehend relationship for relationship's sake. However, Jesus' life on earth gives us a window into that relationship. He did not do or say anything without the Father's direction. God's intrinsically relational being makes Him God. This is not an attribute but who He is.

> As soon as Jesus was baptized, he went up out of the water. At that moment heaven was opened, and he saw the Spirit of God descending like a dove and alighting on him. And a voice from heaven said, "This is my Son, whom I love; with him I am well pleased." (Matthew 3:16–17)

The first time God validated Jesus, He identified Him with a relational definition—"my Son." God did not say Jesus was a healer, miracle worker, provider, or even Savior. He defined who Jesus was, not what He had come to do. God the Father, God the Son, and God the Holy Spirit have an intrinsic relational character of being. Their doing is an overflow of their being.

Humanity is the evidence of God's extrinsic relational nature. The image of God in us shows that He desires a relationship with us. Only we human beings can have a personal relationship with God Himself. This demonstrates the relational identity of God.

God, who is Spirit, desires to have a relationship of love with us. Understanding that, not as a belief but as an experiential reality, is a game-changer!

This has nothing to do with the religion of Christianity, Hinduism, Islam, Buddhism, or any other religion that human beings have created. God, living in humanity through the cross of Christ, is available to everyone.

THE IDENTITY OF GOD'S ENEMY

Just as God exists, so does His enemy, known as Satan, Lucifer, the Accuser, as well as other names. God had no beginning. He is the beginning and the end (Revelation 22:13). But the Enemy had a beginning and has a definite end. No one created God, for He is the self-existent One, but the Enemy is a created being that went wrong. Lucifer was originally part of the kingdom of God and, through his rebellion, chose to become God's foe.

> How you have fallen from heaven, morning star, son of the dawn! You have been cast down to the earth, you who once laid low the nations! You said in your heart, "I will ascend to the heavens; I will raise my throne above the stars of God; I will sit enthroned on the mount of assembly, on the utmost heights of Mount Zaphon. I will ascend above the tops of the clouds; I will make myself like the Most High." (Isaiah 14:12–14)

Satan lost his personal and corporate identities, so he created a kingdom identity of his own. This is why he became known as a thief. This is not a description of his character but who he is. Therefore, throughout history he has worked to accomplish three things in every life God has created:

1. Kill personal identity
2. Steal relational identity
3. Destroy kingdom identity

Jesus distinguished His intent from Satan's, saying, "The thief comes only to steal and kill and destroy; I have come that they may have life, and have it to the full" (John 10:10).

The Enemy had a personal identity—the "morning star" and the "son of the dawn" (Isaiah 14:12). But Satan did not choose to keep the identity given him at creation. He wanted a different one.

Satan rebelled because he wanted to be like God. Essentially, he had an identity crisis. His identity as the Enemy was born from a desire to be like

God. But he wouldn't be satisfied to have the identity of God. He wanted an identity *above* God. The Enemy desired preeminence over God.

This desire is not an attribute of the Enemy; it *is* the Enemy. Therefore, there is no good and no truth in Satan. His desire for another identity gave birth to that which exists to rob our identities. The Enemy's core purpose is to "steal, kill, and destroy" identity.

The Enemy exists in the spiritual realm, in the invisible. He is a person, a creation, and a being, not an idea or an act of the imagination. He is not simply a metaphor for evil but rather the reality of evil.

God cast down the Enemy because Satan planned to invade Heaven, to sit on a throne above God's, and to manage the Creator. The Enemy wanted to replace God as the I Am. The essence of evil attempted to replace the One who is good.

> For such people are false apostles, deceitful workers, masquerading as apostles of Christ. And no wonder, for Satan himself masquerades as an angel of light. It is not surprising, then, if his servants also masquerade as servants of righteousness. Their end will be what their actions deserve. (2 Corinthians 11:13-15)

Even today, the Enemy seeks to replace God. That is who he is in his sole purpose. The Enemy's character, strategy, and attributes, all that he intends and accomplishes, are centered on this core goal—to replace God. This is the being of the Enemy. Replacing God with possessions and things that are destructive is common knowledge; what we need to understand in the times that we live now is the enemy's ability to look like God. Discerning Christian leaders from those actually sent by the Enemy requires great wisdom. Satan coming in the form of an angel of light is not easy to recognize. But this recognition comes when we are in relationship with the Light.

> You belong to your father, the devil, and you want to carry out your father's desires. He was a murderer from the beginning, not holding to the truth, for there is no truth

in him. When he lies, he speaks his native language, for he
is a liar and the father of lies. (John 8:44)

Jesus says the devil speaks "his native language"—lies. This is an
amazing description of the Enemy's (the devil) identity. Lying is not an
attribute of the Enemy but who he is. Murder, manipulation, deceit, and
all manner of evil are his inherent nature.

He uses doubt, fear, hate, and temptation to express his identity. Our
own inability to love others, as well as ourselves, comes from this same place.
All evil is centered on the being of the Enemy. If this sounds like a cosmic
theory, like a fairy tale or a figment of imagination, turn on the news. The
cosmic story becomes a reality all too close to home. The historical reality
of this story is evidenced by the present experience of evil all around. This
goes way beyond errors of judgment by human beings.

Examining my own life, I realized I was making mistakes, but there
were also fierce, self-destructive, lustful desires inside me that were difficult
to explain as my own character. I am certainly bad, but some evil is way
beyond me! In today's world, how do we explain killing one another in the
name of God, race, language, and color? In a world of logic and science,
how do we explain an intentional overdose by people who appear to have
everything in life? All irrational behavior is not evil, but there is some that
is very difficult to explain as part of human nature.

Evil is a person, and his name is Satan whose only goal is to keep pushing
humanity into more and more self-destructive behavior. The understanding
of evil as a person is not to excuse ourselves and put the blame on someone
else, but it is so that we understand there is a supernatural world where
counterfeit experiences are manufactured for humanity to consume to keep
us from God.

THE POWER OF ULTIMATE CHOICE

We human beings are unique in our power to choose. Free will is a reflection
of our spirituality. Choice is a powerful human attribute. But this power is
not actually a choice. When we are born, we do not choose choice but are

born with this ability. If there is one present attribute of human beings that reflects the original design, it is the power to choose.

For those of us who desire absolute freedom, choice teaches that we do not have the choice to choose. We are not free to choose choice but are slaves of choice! We can never be free from choices, and we know this makes life beautiful and destructive all at the same time. Without choices, humanity would have been just an extremely intelligent robot.

The human ability to make choices is unique:

- Beyond brain function
- Beyond the rational
- Contrary to the logic of reason
- Counter to our instincts

Only spiritual beings have this exclusive power of ultimate choice. A fish can never choose to live on land, but people can choose to live in water. A lion could never choose to explore outer space, but people can. All other creatures have choices programmed into their DNA. A male lion stays a male lion because he was born into that state. But men and women even have the power to choose how they will express their sexuality. A human being has the freedom of choice in response to any external stimuli. A great example of this is how a person can be in identical circumstances at two separate times and make different choices, even with the same stimuli occurring in both instances.

The human DNA explains many actions and attributes, but DNA does not define the human will. God desired volitional choice for humanity. Therefore, the greatest expression of love for a human being is voluntarily choosing God. Human beings were part of the group of created spiritual beings who could voluntarily choose God. Satan, along with one-third of the angels, chose to attempt to dethrone God. The faithful angels stood as a testimony against Lucifer and his cohorts. Humans were intended for the same choice.

There is great beauty in voluntarily loving others. This incredible experience exists in choosing to love others for who they are and not for what they do, give, or possess. Adam and Eve made the choice of going against God's instructions, and the consequences are where we find ourselves.

Today, humanity can choose against the instructions of the Enemy and reset life to the original design.

THE GRAND DESIGN

Design precedes action, and once action is taken based on that design, the design takes permanent form. For example, an architect designs a house. When the builders construct the home according to the architect's plan, that design becomes permanently affixed.

The design of humanity in the original creation was God's ultimate expression of Himself. God left His image in human beings so they could live in an exclusive communion of love and intimacy with Him. The spiritual dimension in human beings is part of our basic design. We can deny, ridicule, or ignore this truth, but the fact remains that God and humanity have an exclusive relationship so we are fundamentally designed for spiritual communion, communication, and companionship. This has nothing to do with religion or belief. This is who we are. We need to remind ourselves that there was no faith, religion, or creed in the original design. God and humanity were as connected as gasoline to an engine.

Plants have a unique capacity for expression, but there is an invisible connection between the root system and the soil. The transfer of water and nutrients from the soil to the plant through the root system sustains the plant. There is a beautiful dependence in the independence of plants.

The days are coming when a car will be covered with photovoltaic cells that will capture the sun's energy and convert it into electric energy that will drive the software that will then drive the car—a seamless transfer of energy from the sun to the car. The car is independent. The sun is independent. But a beautiful relationship between the two will enable the software to power the car's hardware. Likewise, the life of God through His Spirit rebirths the human spirit and powers the human mind, which drives the human body—an incredible display of communion and intimacy with God.

When we look at nature, we never see a cow and a horse fighting over whether to worship at a mosque or temple? But turn on the TV or read a newspaper and you'll see the greatest displays of hatred and bloodshed on the planet over race and religion. How in the world can we kill one another based on what we believe? Murder over religious differences has continued through the centuries. The names of Yahweh, Jesus, Allah, and Ram have been the greatest sources of conflict in the world.

If we were the result of the Big Bang or evolution, we might expect that the process of natural de-selection would have removed the stupidity of killing one another over religion by now. Evolution should have transformed our brains to make progressively better choices. In fact, monkeys have far greater communal harmony than homo sapiens do today! The greatest bloodbaths still occur over faith or the lack thereof. The sooner we grasp the fact that we are far more than mere flesh and blood, the easier it will be to understand who we are, why we are here, and who we can become.

The "I" of humanity was originally powered by the "I Am" of God. Human beings were able to give because they received. They experienced love and were able to love. They experienced peace and were able to be at peace with themselves and one another. The design of God was for human beings to draw all their resources from Him so they could then share these resources with the outside world. Human autonomy was powered by a relationship with God. The independence of mankind was powered by interdependence with God.

Just as an automobile engine cannot operate without gasoline, we cannot operate without being reconnected to the Source. Adam and Eve experienced an inner rest that never required searching and seeking. They secured their self-worth and self-esteem through this inner constant that defined their identity. This is also who we were and who we are meant to become.

We are indeed the grandest and greatest of all creations, for we have the dimension of God Himself! This was the original design by our loving Abba Father!

I want to close this section with a challenge.

Take a few minutes to look inside yourself. Allow no other voices or external noise. Spend time in total silence and you will sense an inner reality beyond the mind and body that will confirm you are far more than flesh and blood. Take time to pick up that inner cosmic signal that is always there, telling you there is something more to life. Irrespective of external variables of good and bad, there is an inner cosmic constant in all of humanity that desires to return to our original design.

Part III
Fallen Creation

And the Lord God commanded the man, "You are free to eat from any tree in the garden; but you must not eat from the tree of the knowledge of good and evil, for when you eat from it you will certainly die." (Genesis 2:16–17)

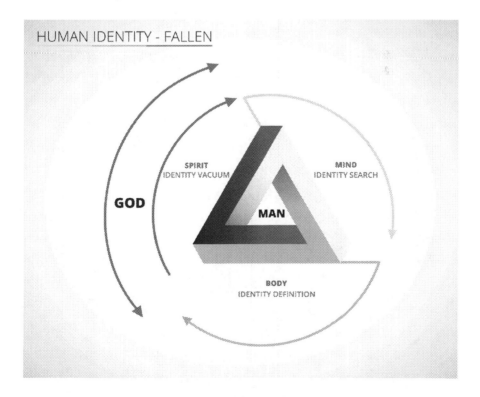

HUMAN IDENTITY - FALLEN

SPIRIT
IDENTITY VACUUM

MIND
IDENTITY SEARCH

GOD

MAN

BODY
IDENTITY DEFINITION

THE DISTORTED ORIGINAL

- ✦ How did we lose the original design?
- ✦ What happened when we lost the original design?
- ✦ Who did we become?
- ✦ How are we trying to regain the original?
- ✦ What key indicators demonstrate our design faults to us?

God, Lucifer, Adam, and Eve, all with unique identities, are the central personalities in the original story of life. Lucifer's goal was to dethrone God. Unable to accomplish the coup and cast out of Heaven, Lucifer went after God's creation—Adam and Eve.

We've seen this plot in countless movies—if you can't hit the father, hurt his kids. If you can't overthrow the king, go after his kingdom. As much as we want to deny the reality of a destructive supernatural world (Satan) and the unexplainable destructive reality in mankind (sin), as much as we want to wish these away as cosmic mythology, we all know an inexplicable evil is bent on destruction within us and around us.

The twenty-first-century mind finds it hard to understand or accept this cosmic war zone. Even if we are unable to comprehend the historical reality of creation, God, and Satan, the reality we now face points to the stories about them in Scripture. If we could accept the reality of God, Satan, and sin, not only could we make sense of the world around us, but we would also find a way out of the cosmic black hole inside us, which is an incredible way to live life.

Without internal personal harmony, there can be no external communal harmony. When we experience transformation from our inner emptiness, historical stories would then become objective evidences. The only way we can truly understand these stories is to experience the reality of Christian spirituality. Far too many voices ask us to believe in Christian history without providing *present* evidence for Christ's reality.

We can offer philosophical, scientific, and psychological explanations for how the innocence of childhood is transformed into the most fearful actions of adulthood, but we all acknowledge that the reality of evil goes beyond just bad intentions. How did this good and evil streak in humanity come about? Why are we unable to consistently keep away from evil? How is it possible for people to kill in the name of religion or defend their "spiritual beliefs" through violence? Why does our best intent and actions not release the worst of our inner emptiness?

We see a systematic destruction of the original design for humanity in what happened to the perfect relationship between God, Adam, and Eve. The destruction of the relationship between the Master Designer and His grandest design was the biggest blow to happen to humanity, resulting in the natural dimension where we now find ourselves. This eternal devastation involved four elements:

- Personal identity (the realm that defined Adam and Eve as individuals)
- Privilege identity (the work that Adam and Eve did)
- Corporate identity (Adam and Eve in their life together)
- Kingdom identity (the dominion of God in Adam and Eve)

This resulted in the translocation of the human race in what we experience now as the fallen creation in a fallen world. The human spirit, mind, and body were distorted from their original design. The choice of listening to the Enemy completely altered who we are, what we experience, and how we behave.

Separation from the original design changed our structure. Once equally spirit, mind, and body, we became just mind and body with a spiritual vacuum. After operating only from our spiritual core, we now operate from the mind. Our identity was once defined in the realm of the spirit but is now defined in the realm of the mind and the body. Once spiritual beings with flesh and blood, we became flesh and blood with a rudimentary spiritual dimension.

Understanding the change in design that the Enemy caused individually and corporately in humanity and the damage that has been done is critical to experiencing the disruption of the cross of Jesus. We are far removed from how we were supposed to live, how we should relate to one another, and how our environment was supposed to be. The good news is that all this can change and we can start the journey of experiencing the original that gives us evidence in the present for a future of perfection for which we all long.

As we move forward in this section, two constant themes will be the damage inflicted by the Enemy and humanity's consistent attempt to duplicate God to fill the inner cosmic vacuum. But emptiness will never be the solution to emptiness, and darkness will never be the solution to darkness.

The Beginning of the End: The Experience of Doubt

The identity thief entered the garden and engaged the woman:

> Now the serpent was more crafty than any of the wild animals the Lord God had made. He said to the woman, "Did God really say, 'You must not eat from any tree in the garden'?" The woman said to the serpent, "We may eat fruit from the trees in the garden, but God did say, 'You must not eat fruit from the tree that is in the middle of the garden, and you must not touch it, or you will die.'" "You will not certainly die," the serpent said to the woman. "For God knows that when you eat from it your eyes will be opened, and you will be like God, knowing good and evil." (Genesis 3:1–5)

Notice the Enemy's first question: "Did God really say …?"

This is a question that human beings would have to answer in perpetuity. Did God really say that? Did God really mean that? Would God actually communicate that? Can God actually do that?

Doubt—questioning God—is the seed this event sowed in humanity. The doubts we experience today are the evidence of a historical reality that keeps us from seeing the other side of the coin—experiencing God. Doubt and experiencing God are polar opposites. The Enemy injected his venom so human beings would forever struggle with faith that leads to experiencing God.

Doubt is not a part of who we were or who we were meant to be. Philosophers, scholars, scientists, and even theologians often base their careers on the question of the existence and nonexistence of God. The seed is indeed planted deep in all of us.

Notice the claim the Enemy makes in Genesis 3: "You will not certainly die." First comes the question to raise doubt; second comes a statement totally contradicting God. Creating a barrier that breaks the relationship between God and humanity was the Enemy's plan from the beginning. He did not want mankind to be in the divine state of completeness but to be in a state of restlessness like him. The Enemy knew that if the Spirit-to-spirit relationship were severed, the objective of influencing and controlling humanity would be achieved.

Contradiction—forever planted—is not part of who we were or who we were meant to be. Countless books, speeches, dissertations, debates, and discussions have brought arguments regarding the existence and nonexistence of God. Contradicting truth is the present evidence to a historical reality.

Lastly, the Enemy redefines human identity: "You will be like God."

This was the knockout punch. Doubt and contradiction were only body jabs. The real assault was on the personal identity of human beings. The Enemy knew that if he could get mankind to accept this desire to be like God, all other elements of creation would also fall. Humanity's desire to become God, kill Him, or replace Him is the present evidence to a historical reality.

This was not just a nail *in* the coffin; it was the hammer blow that created the need *for* a coffin!

DEATH'S BIRTHDAY

That phrase sounds contradictory, but death had to be born in order to exist, as it was not part of the original vocabulary for humanity.

> And the Lord God commanded the man, saying, "You are free to eat from any tree in the garden; but you must not eat from the tree of the knowledge of good and evil, for when you eat from it you will certainly *die*." (Genesis 2:16–17)

Notice what God told Adam and Eve before the Enemy showed up: "for when you eat of it you will certainly *die*."

> Altogether, Adam lived a total of 930 years, and *then he died*. (Genesis 5:5)

If Adam lived for 930 years, then what died in him on the day he ate the fruit? Understanding and comprehending the answer to this question is what differentiates the cross of Christ from all the religions and philosophies of the world. The spiritual realm that enabled Adam to have a relationship with God died instantly, while the body took many years to die. The realm that ensured the absence of the cosmic vacuum died. The fall of humanity and the beginning of the present state started with the death of the spiritual faculty in mankind that could be in communion, communication, and companionship with God. The dimension beyond mind and body that could communicate with God died. Consequently, death occurred in all realms. While spiritual death was the cause, physical death was the consequence. Supernatural beings became natural beings. The ability of human beings to live in constant community and intimacy with God died.

They lost the ability to:

- Experience their identity as children of God
- Live in perfect love relationships within the community
- Live forever in the body

In the military, if the command center is hit, all other units are cut off and become ineffective. When a computer's operating system is infected with a virus, all the programs will crash. In the same way, humanity lost its ability to experience the awareness of God. Humanity was birthed in the original with a cognitive ability to be aware of God. Spiritual death brought the demise of this awareness. This state resulted in the recognition of inner emptiness, along with the birth of the desire to fill that inner spiritual vacuum with things from the dimensions of the mind and body. There is a cosmic vacuum that we try to fill with material things.

When plants run out of water, they can no longer absorb the nutrients in the soil and so they die. But when humanity lost its unique connection to the supernatural, it started the journey of trying to fill the supernatural with the natural.

The death of the body is an event, while the death of the spirit is a state. Human beings are now born into this dead state of the spirit. The human dimension that had the ability to live in communion with God has been disconnected from Him. The human operating system is disabled. The spiritual core that defined human identity has been cut off. A chasm formed between the Spirit of God and the spirit of mankind, causing the search for replacements.

Loss of identity, communion, relationship, and intimacy with God are all consequences of the death of the spirit dimension of mankind. Humanity lost its core dimension of design and operation. From being spiritual, humanity became seekers of—or deniers of—the spiritual. From a spiritual being defining our identity, human "doings," not beings, started to define identity solely through the mind and body.

DEATH: THE CHOICE OF HUMANITY

Eternity had been the original plan for humanity. Death was a choice, not a requirement. It was an option under only one circumstance, and Adam and Eve were given the free will to choose between life and death. If God had not given human beings this free choice, they would have been just extremely intelligent robots. The study of the field of AI—artificial intelligence—is an amazing reflection of the God-particle inside all humanity.

True love relationships are based on choice. God did not and will not override this function in human beings. Just as they voluntarily decided not to choose God, we would now have to voluntarily decide to choose God!

There was the tree of life and also the tree that would give Adam and Eve knowledge of good and evil. They were given the choice to do anything—except to eat from the tree that would offer the knowledge of good and evil. Take a moment to consider and connect with these important statements:

+ Choice exists only when there are options to choose from.
+ There is no slavery when there is no freedom.
+ There is no freedom if there is no slavery.
+ If there are no rules, there is no concept of punishment.

Absolute freedom is actually absolute slavery. If there is no freedom, slavery becomes freedom. When there is total freedom, there are no options, and no options mean slavery. Ironically, our desire for total freedom is one of the greatest evidences of our spiritual design. When humanity gains absolute freedom, allowing anyone to do anything irrespective of the consequences for the individual and the community, we will have reached the ultimate state of slavery.

The personal, communal, and moral destructions taking place in the name of freedom today have placed the world in a downward spiral. True freedom exists when we have choices to make and we voluntarily choose the original instead of the duplicates.

The Uniqueness of Knowing Good and Evil

The choice before the fall was not between good and evil but whether to obey what God said or go against Him. There was no moral choice of good and bad for Adam and Eve, for they did not know the difference. Theirs was a pure love relationship where Adam and Eve had to just listen and live by what their Father told them.

> In the middle of the garden were the tree of life and the tree of the knowledge of good and evil. And the Lord commanded the man, "You are free to eat from any tree in the garden; but you must not eat from the tree of the knowledge of good and evil, for when you eat of it you will certainly die." (Genesis 2:9, 16–17)

God's instruction not to eat applied only to the fruit of the tree that would allow Adam to know good and evil. When the Enemy came to Eve, he did not tempt her to eat from the tree of life. He was not concerned about the good things God had ordained to bless humanity. The Enemy's goal was to destroy Adam and Eve's position as children of God by leading them to do what God had forbid them to do. The Enemy wanted to kill the influence of God and introduce his own over humanity.

The Enemy's purpose was to bring humanity down to the state of knowing good and evil. Satan knew that when human beings experienced evil, they would be disconnected from God, just as he was. From then on, because of the disconnected spiritual state of humans, they would not have the power to consistently choose good over evil.

When they chose to go against God, Adam and Eve were exposed to a situation they were not wired to handle. When the Spirit-to-spirit relationship with God died, the mind and body of mankind was exposed to an ecosystem for which they were not originally designed.

The fallen creation from which we now live is not our original home. We are aliens and strangers in a world that was never meant to be our destination. We spend billions of dollars searching for extraterrestrial life; not realizing we are actually the aliens and what we are searching for is the original human being. We cannot use a Band-Aid to cover a bullet hole! There is a fundamental rewiring that must occur to take us back home through the simplicity of Jesus' work on the cross.

Adam and Eve's choice between heeding and disregarding what God said is the same one we are given every day.

Christianity is about a choice of restoring the original from what God says to become versus what the Enemy says to do to keep us in the present. Jesus is not in the business of moral and behavioral alteration. Character transformation is an effect and not a cause in Christianity. Behavioral transformation is only the result of inner transformation. There is a fundamental spiritual and cognitive rewiring that occurs in us to take us back home through the simplicity of Christ's work on the cross.

Our core problem today is not our actions. We think bad behavior is the issue and desperately try to create religious rules to change this. But the true problem is our fallen state, which has left us unable to be in a relationship with God that goes beyond mere belief. Everything else is only a consequence of this alien state in which we find ourselves.

DEATH'S CONSEQUENCE: RELATIONSHIP LOST, CONFLICT FOUND

Relationship with God is the fundamental design for humanity—life lived inside out. Adam lost his position as a son and Eve her position as a daughter when they lost their ability to live in communion with God. Relationship first, position second. When the faculty that could relate to God—the spirit—died, so did their position as children of God. Relational death was the cause; positional death was the consequence. The dimension in mankind that could commune with God died. This led to the death of the relationship with God, which led to the death of the position as a child of God. Because of this, there is a sequential inside-out destruction that takes place in humanity.

> The man said, "The woman you put here with me—she gave me some fruit from the tree, and I ate it." (Genesis 3:12)

The loss of relationship with God brought about another tragedy. Adam had viewed Eve as "flesh of my flesh" and had been one with her, but suddenly she looked different to him. From "Wow, man!" to "Whoa! Man." Essentially, Adam told God, "The problem is this woman you stuck me with!" Self-centeredness reigned, quickly becoming "every 'man' for himself."

Broken communion with God produced broken communion with Eve. Adam now viewed Eve as a third party. Once a blessing and someone of suitability, she became a burden and something to blame, someone to use and abuse. This loss of human identity meant a broken relationship with God and a broken relationship between Adam and Eve.

> Now Cain said to his brother Abel, "Let's go out to the field." While they were in the field, Cain attacked his brother Abel and killed him. Then the Lord said to Cain, "Where is your brother Abel?" "I don't know," he replied. "Am I my brother's keeper?" (Genesis 4:8–9)

Human conflict now extended beyond the generation of Adam and Eve, becoming the new identity of the fallen creation. The love relationship with God was broken. The human love relationship was broken. The loss of personal identity gave birth to corporate conflict. Disunity was a direct consequence of the loss of personal identity. When there is no experience of Christ's sonship identity, there is disunity!

SIN'S BIRTHDAY

> Therefore, just as sin entered the world through one man, and death through sin, and in this way death came to all people, because all sinned. (Romans 5:12)

> For the flesh desires what is contrary to the Spirit, and the Spirit what is contrary to the flesh. They are in conflict with each other, so that you are not to do whatever you want. (Galatians 5:17)

Death in the realm of the spirit is not death, as we know it, but rather the deactivation of the spirit. Removed from the dominion of God and under the dominion of the Enemy, this dead state of the spirit in humanity is sin. Spiritual death put mankind in an ecosystem called sin. Sin is a state of being and not a status of doing. We are not sinful because we do wrong, but we do wrong because we are sinful. A person who is not in Spirit-to-spirit communion with God exists in this state called sin. Even if any man or woman should be perfect in thought and action, they would still not have a relationship with God because humanity is born into an ecosystem called sin. So sin is not what we do; it is who we are in this spiritually disconnected state.

From an ecosystem of wholeness, we were translocated to an ecosystem of unholiness. The first murder was not the cause of sin, but sin was the cause of the first murder. This sequence is not semantics but one that differentiates religion from relationship.

This creates a progressive implication in mankind. Death of the spirit is the cause; the state of sin is the effect. This state of sin is the cause; sinful nature is the effect. Sinful nature is the cause; sinful desires are the effects. Sinful desire is the cause; sinful actions are the result. The disease is sin, while the symptoms are sinful actions.

Our sinful nature—the tendency in humanity toward all things against God—is experienced in the mind but expressed through the body. We think wrong thoughts; therefore, we take wrong actions. The state of sin encourages us to desire evil.

There is no need to teach human beings to desire evil things. In fact, the attraction to do evil grows as the mind and body grow. This is exactly why we refer to the innocence of a child but not of an adult. The intensity of this desire varies among human beings, but it is present on some level in all people. For example, no one needed to teach me to pick up the cigarette that my dad threw away. My brother, on the other hand, who grew up in the same circumstances, never picked one up.

Though circumstances play a great role in human behavior, fundamental inner design faults are far more influential. The reasons for my behavior involve much more than my environment or my lack of self-worth. I am wired to go after all that my mind, body, and the world around me tell me to pursue. I am constantly responding to these forces, for that is the state in which I live. My desires are triggered through visual and sensory windows of the mind and body. The triggers are as varied as the desires themselves.

My mind, under the sinful state's total control, is unable to consistently filter out the bad and keep doing the good. My mind, as a slave to my sinful state, is unable to consistently overcome internal and external triggers.

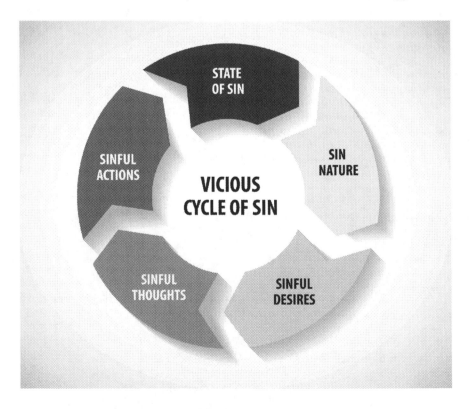

SIN IN WORLD RELIGIONS

Sin is not solely a Judeo-Christian concept. Many religions speak of humanity's sin and sinful nature. The following Hindu texts, written hundreds of years before Christ, illustrate a longing for purity and a desire for freedom from sin.

> Shining brightly, Agni [fire], drive away
> our sin, and shine wealth on us.
> Shining bright, drive away our sin.
> For good fields, for good homes, for wealth,
> we made our offerings to Thee.
> Shining bright, drive away our sin ...
> So that Agni's conquering beams
> may spread out on every side,
> Shining bright, drive away our sin.
>
> Thy face is turned on every side,
> Thou pervadest everywhere.
> Shining bright, drive away our sin.
> —Rig Veda 1.97.1–6

> Of the sin against the gods Thou art atonement;
> Of the sin against men Thou art atonement;
> Of the sin against myself Thou art atonement;
> Of every kind of sin Thou art atonement.
> The sin that I have committed knowingly,
> and that I have committed unawares,
> of all sins Thou art atonement.
> —Yajur Veda 8.13

"*Papokam, papa kanmokam, papathma papa samphava; thrahimam Pundarikaksha sarva papa hari hare.*" (I am born in sin, doer of sin, and a sinful self; I am the worst of all sinners. Lord, save me from all my sins.) (Rig Veda 7.86.3)

The Brihad Aranyaka Upanishad says that the *jeeva* (soul) acquires evil at birth (4.3.8).

"*Rog Sog Dhuk Paritab Bhandan Vyasnanicha, Aatma aparatha Vrukshanam phalarh edhani dehinam*" is a common saying that means "What are the fruits of this sinful tree which is our body?" They are "sickness, sorrow, pain, bondage, and many other kinds of sins." No one is free from the bondage of sin.

Islamic scriptures also illustrate a desire for forgiveness.

"They said: 'O our father! Ask forgiveness [from Allah] for our sins; indeed we have been sinners'" (Qur'an Yusuf 12:97–16). "Those who say: 'Our Lord! We have indeed believed, so forgive us our sins and save us from the punishment of the Fire'" (Qur'an Aal-Imran 3:16).

"Shall I not seek forgiveness? O Allah, You are my Lord, there is no God but You; for You created me and I am Your servant; and I am upon Your covenant and Your promise as much as I am able; I seek refuge in You from the evil of what I have done; I acknowledge Your favors upon me and I recognize my sins, so forgive my sins; verily, none can forgive sins but You" (Sunan at-Tirmidhi, Book of Supplications, Number 3393, Hasan).

Even Buddhism expresses "*Akusala, mula,*" a concept of unwholesomeness or a lack of skill.

People seeking after God have had revelations concerning the reality of sin and have expressed this truth in various ways in many religions. Only in the Bible is the reason for our dichotomous and circumstantial behavior not only explained but also resolved. All religions agree on the concept of sin and its effects, but the Bible alone explains the *why* of sin and the solution to experiencing freedom from it. Holiness or wholeness cannot be achieved by going to church, a temple, or mosque. Doing the right things does not make us holy. This is why even after doing the right things, or at the heights of *dharma* from Hinduism and Buddhism, inwardly we still long for something more. Actions, activities, and locations do not produce holiness.

Holiness is an inner state of awareness we experience when we are in a spiritual relationship with God that consequentially leads to transformation of the mind expressing the character of God, which is wholeness through our bodies. Holiness is an inner spiritual relational journey that the mind recognizes and the body expresses.

CONDEMNATION

For humanity, guilt is a constant reality resulting in condemnation. Guilt and condemnation are present realities that evidence a historical truth. Even when everything is going well, we still feel bad. Even in so-called perfect relationships, we encounter imperfect problems. Why do we have a sense of condemnation even in perfect situations?

When the Spirit-to-spirit relationship with God was broken, humanity entered a state of sin, and the consequence was condemnation. This is not a consequence of what we do, but of who we have become. Condemnation is a state-of-mankind problem, not a state-of-mind problem. We are in an ecosystem of sin, which brings condemnation. The physical setting does not influence this sense of condemnation, and we know by present experience that our best behavioral actions and our present "ideal" circumstances do not get us out of this either. Using the power of the mind to control the mind and body can only get us so far but would not fill a deeper spiritual need that can be experienced only through an inter-dimensional interplay of spirit, mind, and body.

Even in a perfect situation, emptiness exists as a result of condemnation. This is the most frustrating experience for humanity. In the midst of physical and intellectual perfection, there is an imperfection we all know deep inside us. Our greatest efforts are to stay in a state of internal contentment in the midst of external contentment, which is a unique human paradox. The perfect weather, perfect company, perfect physical setting, and perfect intellectual achievement do not equal a perfect inner state of the mind. Holy places and holy actions will never deliver us from internal guilt and condemnation.

> Whoever believes in the Son has eternal life, but whoever rejects the Son will not see life, for God's wrath remains on them. (John 3:36)

Not only are we in a state of condemnation, but our fallen identity also places us under God's wrath. We can never truly comprehend or appreciate the cross until we understand our position and condition before God. In rebellion and under God's wrath, we are separated from Him, experiencing the punishment this ecosystem brings. The more we try to resolve this spiritual issue in the mind and body, the further down we spiral. Born into this state of separation from God, we bear the greatest pain we can experience. Hell is separation from God. We know this and experience it daily, struggling to find peace and love, irrespective of wealth or poverty.

From Genesis 3 to the final chapter of Revelation, the story of the Bible is about humanity's spiritually disconnected state and the consequences of the Enemy's work and the God of the universe calling us to get back to the original. Human beings were thrust into a dimension where they were never created to exist. Their supply line was cut off, so they chose to build their own.

When human beings disobeyed God, they underwent a foundational change. Sin gave birth to a new creature. After sin, Adam and Eve were totally different beings in terms of their identity, structure, and function.

The Spiritual Vacuum

The death of the spirit, the birth of sin, a sinful nature, and sinful desires led human beings to lose personal identity gained through communion with God in the spirit. A sense of helplessness that could not be relieved by the mind or body now existed.

Our changed spiritual state creates a vacuum that causes us to long for something more. No source outside God will meet our need. In this orphaned condition, fallen creation seeks any and every solution, but none satisfies in a sustainable way.

> "You are a child of the devil and an enemy of everything
> that is right! You are full of all kinds of deceit and trickery.
> Will you never stop perverting the right ways of the Lord?"
> (Acts 13:10)

When humanity lost its capacity to commune with God, the Father-and-child relationship that defined the personal identity of human beings was destroyed. The intimacy, communion, and embrace between the heavenly Father and His children ended, placing humanity in a spiritual vacuum. We now have a spiritual antenna that is sweeping the cosmos for an authentic supernatural relationship. There is a constant search going on inside us all, irrespective of how much we may have already found or not found in terms of possessions and power.

This state is like gravity, which does not need our permission to exist. When a child is conceived, the spirit is also co-conceived in the womb. The mind and the body develop there, but the spirit stays rudimentary. Here, the spirit is open to the influence of the Enemy as the child matures and becomes aware.

None of us can escape this realm beyond the mind and body. In this confused and distorted state, we seek meaning and purpose to life beyond the tangible world. With the destruction of personal identity, even after we achieve great success, that emptiness in the spirit returns quickly with a vengeance. This eternal hangover of humanity exists because of the broken relationship between God and mankind.

Human beings struggle inside a theistic vacuum. No other living being needs to wrestle with this spiritual dilemma. With the death of the spirit, we now attempt to find our purpose in what we do.

My business ventures have convinced me of the greatness involved in inventions, innovations, and achievements. But we should not be fooled into thinking these earthly successes will give us what we seek internally.

When our internal communion with God ended, the consequences were clearly visible. The way we approach God, one another, and creation has changed. As a result, what we think is natural is actually unnatural, what we have assumed to be normal is actually abnormal, and our idea of God could not actually be God!

THE GAP OF DEATH

All things that die go through a transformation process that is not instantaneous. A seed in the soil lies dormant for growth later, absorbing moisture and nutrients to grow, or it dies. Death brings a process of decay. The molecular structures break down, other external microorganisms feed on it, and death is eventually seen on the outside. This is true of all living things.

Loss of life leads to death. Then the disintegration process expresses the internal death externally. The time between death and its expression is called the gap of death. From the time humanity lost its original design of living in a spiritual relationship with God, it has been in a process of great transformation in its expressions of inner reality of the loss of life.

Unlike any other creature, humanity is able to live physically without its original Source of life. Even though we are dead spiritually, we are alive in the mind and body. This is exactly why seeking the fountain of youth and immortality is as old as human civilization. The spirituality inside us desperately desires and seeks immortality. Duplicity of religious expressions is the external expression of an internal death state. Through the centuries, these have changed based on culture, politics, and economic progress while the religion called Christianity has its own expressions as well.

Key Death Indicators in Twenty-First-Century Christianity

When the expressions and behaviors of Christianity become the primary evidence, we have *created* the religion called Christianity. Christian behavior is possible without having Christ, but it is impossible to have Christ and not have Christlike behavior. There is a major difference between these. When we define our Christian identity by what we do, we belong to a religion called Christianity.

Through the next section, we will outline thirteen Key Death Indicators (KDIs) of Christian behavior that line up more with the fallen creation than with original design. These will help us contrast the major differences between the religion of Christianity and having a relationship with Christ.

Key Death Indicator 1: Identity Confusion

"Very truly I tell you, whoever believes in me will do the works I have been doing, and they will do even greater things than these, because I am going to the Father. And I will do whatever you ask in my name, so that the Father may be glorified in the Son. You may ask me for anything in my name, and I will do it." (John 14:12–14)

Privilege identity is what God does *through* us. Human beings confuse this with what God does *in* us—the transformational experience of sonship identity as a child of God.

For centuries people have developed the ability to do the supernatural in and through the natural realm. This is common in Eastern mysticism, African voodoo, and Latin American shamanism. The physical realm can use the supernatural realm to produce amazing wonders. This is not a relationship but a transaction for financial gain. God is relational. The Enemy is transactional. Just because the name of Jesus is used does not mean Jesus is present. In fact, all too often we find a wolf in sheep's clothing among God's people.

Paul put it this way in 2 Corinthians 2:17: "Unlike so many, we do not peddle the word of God for profit. On the contrary, in Christ we speak before God with sincerity, as those sent from God." The Greek word for *peddle* is *kapeleuo*. This means to sell products or services for a profit. By profession a tent maker, Paul knew what making a profit meant. In fact, through his business profit, he sustained himself and his team in Thessalonica. But when it came to preaching and teaching the Word, he operated on a cost model and not a profit model, as he stated in 1 Timothy 6:5: "And constant friction between people of corrupt mind, who have been robbed of the truth and who think that godliness is a means to financial gain."

> "Many will say to me on that day, 'Lord, Lord, did we not prophesy in your name and in your name drive out demons and in your name perform many miracles?' Then I will tell them plainly, 'I never *knew* you. Away from me, you evildoers!'" (Matthew 7:22–23)

Fallen creation wrongly believes all miraculous displays to be of God. Jesus clearly teaches that supernatural works by themselves do not prove human beings are children of God. We may claim to know Jesus and use His name, but what truly matters is if Jesus knows us (Matthew 7:21–23)! The former is religion; the latter is relationship. Relationship involves two people knowing one another. The religion of Christianity defines "identity" by what we *do* and our *knowledge* of Jesus.

We tend to think that Eastern mysticism and African witch doctors are spiritual counterfeits, but much like these, twenty-first-century Christianity is now predominantly also about the supernatural displayed through the mind and body with no transformational image of Jesus being formed in the individual. If the experience of Jesus' activity ends with a miracle of the mind or body without an ongoing transformational Spirit-to-spirit relational communion, this experience is a counterfeit.

Supernatural eloquence and healing do not prove Christian identity even if they claim the name of Jesus. Because of their fallen nature, human beings mistake the *power* of God for the *Person* of God. They also confuse *what* God does with *who* He is. When the "doings" of God do not lead to the transformational formation of the being of God but keep people in the ever-seeking deception of going after the attributes of God, this is a key death indicator of the fallen creation of humanity.

KEY DEATH INDICATOR 2: THE TWENTY-FIRST-CENTURY PHARISEE

Once fully integrated beings living solely from the spirit, we became divided into spirit, mind, and body. Our homogenous nature was separated into these three compartments. We gained the ability to:

1. Think one thing and then say another
2. Say one thing and then do another
3. Think something, say another, and then do a completely different thing than what we thought or said

We can portray who we are on the outside as totally different from who we are on the inside.

We can display extreme spirituality on the outside while practicing deviant lifestyles on the inside. We can portray ourselves to the world as the most benevolent people but be amazingly greedy on the inside. We can make people laugh while crying on the inside. We can preach the greatest sermons on holiness while viewing pornography in secret. We can attend marriage seminars and then sleep with a total stranger. We can lead worship and then be drowned in alcohol. Hypocrisy is not what we do but who we are and who we have become, a state of being and not a status of doing. We are not hypocrites because we act, but we act because we are hypocrites.

In Ezekiel 10, when God's Presence left the temple, for all practical purposes the temple should have been shut down. When the Person left the temple, the purpose of the temple ceased. But it did not, and the ceremonies, rules, and regulations continued on. The religion of Christianity exists where there are ceremonies every weekend without the relationship with the Person being experienced throughout the week.

The Pharisees were not pro-Baal and did not worship idols. They were pro-Jehovah and promoted the one true God. They were teachers of His ordained law and instructed others in the precepts of Yahweh. They went to the temple every day, serving the religious system. There was some serious Torah-thumping going on during Jesus' life on earth.

So what did Jesus think about the Pharisees and the teachers of the law? How did He deal with these religious leaders? Ironically, He directed some of His harshest words toward them. The one word He consistently used to describe these men was *hypocrites*, which derives from the Greek *hypokrites*, meaning a stage actor, someone playing a role. An actor is someone who pretends to be someone else. There is no personal transformation in actors. Their inner reality is different from their external portrayal. Who they are changes based on situations, circumstances, and external demands.

The Pharisees' lifestyle on the inside did not match their lifestyle on the outside; they had one lifestyle in the synagogue and another at home, one lifestyle when alone and a different one with people. Like spiritual chameleons, they changed who they were based on their environment.

Our true lifestyle is what we practice in private, so if we portray anything else in public, we too are acting. That is hypocrisy. Going from misfits to ministers, we can put on a show to attract people in order to create a following.

Consider social media. Millions use manicured pictures, captions, and 140-character messages to portray their lives as amazing and awesome, though the reality is actually mundane and messy. We consistently project an image of who we are not. That is hypocrisy.

Today, twenty-first-century Pharisees practice circumstantial Christianity. Their peak religious experience comes on Sunday mornings when they give their best performance. They mistake heightened emotion for high-level spirituality. They make the church building, not the body of Christ, the epicenter of faith. They put on a superficial spirituality when they walk into church, and then when they exit drop it at the door like 3-D glasses at a movie theater, only needed for the emotional experience. The evidence of their faith is reading the Bible, praying, attending church, and taking part in spiritual programs. When they do all of these things, they are certain they have a relationship with God and are bound for Heaven. The Pharisees had the same mindset.

Jesus is invited into and kicked out of their lives based on personal preferences. Fallen creation will play God based on individual choice, circumstances, and location. Therefore, Jesus is not invited into the home, and He also cannot go to:

- Work
- Schools
- Universities
- Government
- Neighborhoods
- The marketplace

In this mindset, Jesus is not with us when we are alone. While He is all over the church—in small group study, revival meetings, and the uttermost parts of the earth and the heavens—Jesus is not welcome into our private personal inner world.

The twenty-first-century Pharisees have ensured that Jesus coexists with a lifestyle of drugs, alcohol, illicit sex, and all manner of evil acts. Jesus in this century is like cologne or perfume—we wear Him when we want to and where we want to, and do not notice when the fragrance vanishes, putting Him on again only when we deem it appropriate or necessary.

In Matthew 23:33, Jesus told the first-century Pharisees, the religious leaders of His day, what He very well might also say to the twenty-first-century Pharisees: "You snakes! You brood of vipers! How will you escape being condemned to hell?"

He was letting them know in no uncertain terms that their faith was misplaced and that Heaven would not be their destination unless they turned from their religion to a Spirit-to-spirit relationship.

Today's Pharisees acknowledge a relationship with God just as they would acknowledge a relationship with a pet—in purely emotional terms. They also use a relationship with God like a chameleon uses colors—solely based on the setting and circumstances for survival.

The apostle Paul gives a great description of the twenty-first-century Pharisee—not about the ungodly, but about the ungodliness of the godly:

> But mark this: There will be terrible times in the last days. People will be lovers of themselves, lovers of money, boastful, proud, abusive, disobedient to their parents, ungrateful, unholy, without love, unforgiving, slanderous, without self-control, brutal, not lovers of the good, treacherous, rash, conceited, lovers of pleasure rather than lovers of God—*having a form of godliness but denying its power*. (2 Timothy 3:1–5)

Just like the first-century Pharisees, the twenty-first-century ones define their identity by what they do and where they go. They are Christians because they go to church, lead worship, pay tithes, and become missionaries or ministry leaders.

Key Death Indicator 3: The Legality of Sin

> They exchanged the truth about God for a lie, and worshiped and served created things rather than the Creator—who is forever praised. Amen. ... Although they know God's righteous decree that those who do such things deserve death, they not only continue to do these very things but also approve of those who practice them. (Romans 1:25, 32)

There is no prison for people who do good. The justice system exists for people who do wrong. But we tend to declare that wrong actions are actually right actions—and conversely that right actions are now considered wrong. We have a predisposition to behave the wrong way. If this were not true, we would not have a justice system in place at all.

Consider all the institutions spawned by sinful human nature: law enforcement agencies, military organizations, and the legal system, including attorneys, judges, bailiffs, and the like. Entire industries, professions, and careers—both honorable and illicit—exist only because of sin!

One of the most ugly expressions of our inner state of death is our desire to remove the concept of right and wrong. If we can systematically make all wrongs right, we can remove God from the system—the Enemy's ultimate objective.

When we declare wrong actions no longer wrong, we are attempting to move from a state of sinfulness to a state of holiness based on actions. But our nature also does not allow us to coexist indefinitely with wrong. The way out of this catch-22 is to declare that wrong is now right so we can coexist with the *new* right.

But no matter how far we take this concept, we will not solve our problem of personal identity. We make wholesale changes to the laws and still have murders, suicides, rapes, and all manner of crime, because we cannot escape our inner reality—the state of death. Legality or illegality is not the cause of fear, depression, loneliness, and despair. The void in our inner beings won't go away just because we can freely express our self-determined sexual identities. We can legislate every historical and biblical definition of right and wrong out of the system, but we will not change humanity's desperately destitute inner state.

Sinful actions are a consequence of this state of being; they are not the core problem. Just as the U.S. Supreme Court has legalized same-sex marriage, the majority of the Christian community has fully embraced no-fault divorce. The law of the land does not define sin but can give permission to indulge in sinful activities with no consequences of punishment. Legislation cannot fix the problem of the inner state of sin but can mask the consequences of sinful actions. Legalizing an illicit drug or a version of marriage is not a political or an ideological issue but a declaration of who we have become.

We will see a progressive increase in historical wrongs declared right and historical rights declared wrong. The more we legalize what is wrong as right, the more we are going to realize that wrong actions and activities are not the primary problem. They are only expressions of an inner state that cannot be transformed through any legislation but only through the simplicity of the cross of Christ.

The progression of culture with its "progressive thinking" drives us further to question if liberalizing matters of the mind and body are the answers we truly seek. Neither will progressively adopting a conservative value system solve the inner dilemmas we so desperately seek. Today, religion promotes conservative values as a reflection of Christianity when eastern religions are fundamentally conservative in their ideology as well.

KEY DEATH INDICATOR 4: NATURAL GOOD

While we have well covered fallen creation's propensity for evil and sin, we must also recognize humanity's ability to do good. The Enemy lured human beings toward evil, but they also gained the ability to distinguish good from evil and can do tremendous good. As much as we are aware of evil, we are equally aware of good.

Human beings can be incredibly creative, intelligent, and independently good-natured. We do not need God to do good, because this capacity already exists in us. The goodness of human beings is a reflection of our original design. The present reality reflects a historical reality!

Cultures and societies from time immemorial have designed value systems for better or for worse. But these designs always vary according to geography, context, and culture.

While few will challenge love, peace, caring, and giving, the reasons why we do good vary. The constant is that we are designed to appreciate and do good and, in such goodness, find inner peace. But from *being* good we transition to simply *doing* good so we can therefore *feel* good.

Giving millions of dollars to charity won't drive away inner emptiness. While it would certainly be a good feeling, we must not confuse such an emotion for spirituality. An increase in donations might end physical poverty around the world, but it would not end spiritual poverty of the individual. However, it is incredibly awesome to give and end physical poverty from a place of spiritual plenty.

One of the Enemy's greatest victories has come in making us think our sinful actions are our biggest problem. Thus we desperately try to solve our inner state by the external means of doing good. This is one of the core characteristics of fallen creation. The Enemy knows the power of human beings in spiritual communion with God, so he has created a distraction to keep us attempting to perfect our actions only through the mind and body. The Enemy does not care if we become good as long as we do so without God. His main goal is to block our spiritual connection with God. Our moral reformation is just fine with him—as long as we become "good" by ourselves.

In our fallen state, we do both evil and good because of who we are. The Enemy makes inroads on both fronts—pushing us to engage in more philanthropy, to perform more environmentally friendly acts, to commit to corporate social responsibility, and to build a culture of benevolence. We think we can beat our own nature by promoting good even as we fight to legalize sin. We find many ways to make ourselves feel good by doing good. But the bandages we put on can only stop the bleeding for so long.

Simultaneously, the Enemy also pushes us to do more evil, to turn wrong into right, and to legalize every sinful action so we no longer feel bad. Neither increasing our good works nor papering over evil will fix the fundamental problem we face. Neither of these will reverse what the Enemy originally achieved. What is left is only the emptiness that afflicts us after having done good deeds; the feeling that there is more to life when our sensory experiences end, remains.

KEY DEATH INDICATOR 5: LOCATIONAL SPIRITUALITY

> "Sir," the woman said, "I can see that you are a prophet. Our ancestors worshiped on this mountain, but you Jews claim that the place where we must worship is in Jerusalem." (John 4:19–20)

Spirituality practiced according to location is yet another indicator of humanity's fallen nature. If our spirituality peaks or is displayed solely on Sundays (or whatever day your worship services occur) and then enters a vacuum, disappearing on weekdays, we show ourselves to be part of fallen creation.

Machu Picchu in Peru makes some people feel spiritual. We can find multiple lists online of the most famous spiritual places—locations where people feel their spirituality is heightened.

If certain places and people make one feel more spiritual than at home, the office, or grocery store, this is not spiritual but emotional. Locational spirituality involves the human mind reaching out to the spiritual realm through the emotions.

A visit to a Hindu temple, Muslim mosque, or Christian church would reveal how spiritual people feel in these locations. We do not apply this thinking anywhere else. When we go scuba diving, we do not believe we have become fish. When we fly in an airplane, we do not believe we have become birds. When we visit a zoo, we do not believe we are animals. But when we spend an hour a week inside a church, we believe we are Christians.

Jesus told the woman at the well:

> "Yet a time is coming and has now come when the true worshipers will worship the Father in the Spirit and in truth, for they are the kind of worshipers the Father seeks. God is spirit, and his worshipers must worship in the Spirit and in truth." (John 4:23–24)

Jesus took the location of spirituality to another dimension beyond the mind and body.

KEY DEATH INDICATOR 6: ABUSES AND ADDICTIONS

We tend to ascribe bad behavior to bad people. For example, someone who steals becomes known as a thief and one who kills is known as a murderer. What we do becomes who we are, thus defining our identity. We fail to recognize that who we are results from who we have become. Humanity's dead state creates an extremely powerful and self-destructive vacuum that can lead us to do things we know are harmful but still go about doing all the same.

"When an impure spirit comes out of a person, it goes through arid places seeking rest and does not find it. Then it says, 'I will return to the house I left.' When it arrives, it finds the house swept clean and put in order. Then it goes and takes seven other spirits more wicked than itself, and they go in and live there. And the final condition of that person is worse than the first." (Matthew 12:43–45)

Jesus is explaining how a person cannot be in a theistic vacuum. The human spirit yearns to be filled, and this inner longing is cognitively experienced in the mind. We know how it feels to be alone in the midst of a crowd! People often attempt to influence the mind and body with experiences that might enable them to escape these effects of inner loneliness. When we do not experience what we long for in our inner beings, we try to escape our aloneness by using a substance or an experience that numbs our emotions. We experiment with many things because we are not satisfied with what we have or where we are in life.

People seek external stimuli to heighten their joy. Alcohol use is an example of a temporary superlative experience of the mind and body. When the blood alcohol level exceeds a certain threshold, a chemical release causes reactions in the brain. These substance-induced sensory feelings can numb the natural consequences of spiritual loneliness. We feel we need a chemical additive in the brain to fill our emptiness.

The trigger to fill our inner loneliness could run the gamut from worship music that we play to make us feel good, all the way to cocaine with its extreme physical effects. Both would give a temporal physical relief, but when the effects are gone, we would go right back to the reality of inner emptiness, pushing us to seek the next high. Any source temporarily influencing the mind and body alone can lead to addictions and abuses that do not provide what we are seeking.

Over time, chemicals create patterns of behavior that cause us to crave more. Even success and blessings can become a curse when they fail to fill our emptiness. Many forms of abuse—anger, lust, materialism, greed, jealousy, etc.—arise from our inability to handle the inner vacuum.

When success does not fill an inner longing for the meaning to life, this can be an incredibly painful experience. When we thought all along that a million dollars, a million followers, or a global platform of power and fame would solve our inner emptiness and provide true fulfillment, yet it does not, that overwhelming disappointment and pain needs to be numbed. It is extremely painful to be filled in the mind and body yet still experience inner emptiness. Our mind is confused as to why possessions and power do not satisfy, and then the substances that can temporarily stop that incredible inward cosmic spiral seem to be the only answer.

Human beings long to become complete again and return to their original state. The root cause of all conflicts can be traced back to this vacuum. There is no permanent physical solution to this spiritual problem. The poison injected into human beings by the Enemy corrupted our identity and destroyed our inner spiritual core that defined us.

Fallen creation has always tried to find a way to fill the God-sized vacuum inside, searching for spiritual answers in the realm of the body and mind.

Key Death Indicator 7: Attributes and Actions

> For although they knew God, they neither glorified him
> as God nor gave thanks to him, but their thinking became
> futile and their foolish hearts were darkened. Although
> they claimed to be wise, they became fools and exchanged
> the glory of the immortal God for images made to look like
> a mortal human being and birds and animals and reptiles.
> (Romans 1:21–23)

We human beings also confuse the Person of God with the personality of God. We make the attributes of God into God. This tendency to confuse who He is with what He does is part of our fallen identity. We then seek the actions and the attributes of God, falsely thinking we are seeking God.

The Person of God is different from His personality. Knowing God is different from simply recognizing His attributes. Relating to God is different from relating to His expressed qualities.

A Spirit-to-spirit communion in the original design has now become a mind-to-attribute, emotion-to-attribute, and body-to-attribute transaction.

The God of twenty-first-century Christianity has become only the sum total of His attributes and actions. Our understanding of God starts with what He can do for us, not with who He is and who He can be in us. We say, "Come to Jesus and He will give you peace, wealth, healing, and purpose." Who is this approach about? Us. What is this approach about? One thing: what we can get.

So from all this we have created the religion of Christianity, which encourages us to engage with the attributes of God and believe this is what a relationship with Him means. We may not have created images of gold or silver, but we have certainly created idols.

We engage God only to:

+ Go to Heaven
+ Give us peace
+ Pay our bills
+ Make us feel good
+ Heal our sickness
+ Serve our purposes

We engage with a purpose-driven God to fulfill our own purpose for God on earth!

But engaging with the attributes of God does not require spirituality, because the mind and body can engage with an attribute. Other religions define these and then point people toward them. In Hinduism, Brahma is the equivalent of the Great I Am in Christianity with the expressions of Brahma being various gods and goddesses. For your finances, you can engage with Lakshmi, the goddess of wealth, and this becomes a part of your religious system. There is absolutely no difference between a Hindu praying to Lakshmi for wealth and a Christian praying to Jesus for wealth. There is a vast difference between having a relationship with God and engaging with the attributes of God.

My children can see me as a person or as a set of attributes. When my children see me solely as a financial provider, we do not have a relationship but a transaction-based engagement. But I am more than a set of attributes. When they see me as a father, we have a relationship. I am a father first, and my attributes flow from my fatherhood. I expect my children to relate to me for who I am and not what I give. What I do for them is a consequence of the relational identity between parent and child. My relationship with my children is evidenced by a part of myself in them. DNA evidence is the irrevocable legal proof of fatherhood. Relational evidence is the irreversible proof of my love for them as a dad.

While some may feel I am engaging in semantics here, I am only reflecting Christ's teaching.

> "Not everyone who says to me, 'Lord, Lord,' will enter the kingdom of heaven, but only the one who does the will of my Father who is in heaven. Many will say to me on that day, 'Lord, Lord, did we not prophesy in your name and in your name drive out demons and in your name perform many miracles?' Then I will tell them plainly, 'I never knew you. Away from me, you evildoers!'" (Matthew 7:21–23)

Notice how Jesus distinguished attributes and actions from relationship. He drew a clear line between what is done in His name and knowing Him. In fact, He called the use of His name without a relationship a counterfeit action, an evil. We live in a day where we need to understand that supernatural displays of the miraculous need not be and may not be the evidence of Jesus Christ.

> They exchanged the truth about God for a lie, and worshiped and served created things rather than the Creator. (Romans 1:25)

Paul tells us human beings are constantly making images of creation and mistaking them for God. The creations and expressions of God among humans are not God. The identity of God rests in His self-existence. The evidence of God is known internally and is spiritually discerned. The inner awareness of God in an individual is the evidence of God.

We mistake mere engagements for relationships. A relationship exists at the personal level and not at the action level. Even when actions and attributes fail, a true relationship continues on. When actions and attributes fail or change, an engagement falters or even ends. A performance-based connection is not a real relationship.

True relationship goes beyond actions, attributes, and performance, because it happens at the being level. When we say, "I love you" in today's context, what we are actually saying is, "I love the way you look," "I love the things you have," or "I love the things you do." Again, who are these statements actually about?

> When the people saw that Moses was so long in coming down from the mountain, they gathered around Aaron and said, "Come, make us gods who will go before us. As for this fellow Moses who brought us up out of Egypt, we don't know what has happened to him." (Exodus 32:1)

The Israelites saw God as their deliverer from the slavery of Egypt. They saw Moses as the instrument of that deliverance from their pain and hardship. The Israelites were concerned only with their immediate problems under Pharaoh. When Moses disappeared at Mount Sinai to meet with God, they wanted another deliverer. Their focus was the attribute of deliverance, not the Person of God. So when the person representing the Deliverer was out of their sight, they wanted any god who would help them escape their problems. They did not care who God was. Even though He revealed Himself on Mount Sinai and reached out to them for a relationship, they were interested only in His actions and attributes.

The Israelites' engagement with God was at the level of the mind and body. Their hope was that their desires and immediate problems would be solved through God's actions and attributes. Their engagement was transactional, not relational. God was a quick fix. They did not have a relationship with I Am. As long as He kept meeting their needs, He was a good God. But when problems arose, when life became uncomfortable, the Israelites rebelled. All they cared about was getting to the Promised Land, just as the twenty-first-century religion of Christianity promises Jesus is a passport to Heaven.

The most perverted form of religion is found here—we use God to meet our desires and needs, ever seeking but never understanding (Mark 4:11–12). God becomes another commodity. This is idolatry in twenty-first-century Christianity.

One of the biggest challenges for Christians today is to distinguish between an occasional encounter with God and an ongoing relationship with Him. We must learn the difference between relating to the being of God and engaging with the actions of God. Christians need the wisdom to sift transaction from the relationship. Far too many mind-and-body-experience seekers are fooled into thinking they are in a relationship with God. Religion is public expression that conforms, while relationship is private communion that transforms.

Key Death Indicator 8: From God-Centric to I-Centric

The state of sin replaces my spiritual identity as a child of God with the "I" of the mind and body in humanity. This "I" now becomes my identity independent of God.

"I" defines who I am, which is:

+ What I have
+ What I do
+ How I feel
+ What I possess
+ What I achieve

The "I" takes control under the influence of sinful human nature and becomes master and slave at the same time.

The tragedy of fallen creation is that consciousness becomes human identity. All "I" can think, feel, accomplish, imagine—whatever, whenever, and wherever—is in control and defines identity. Anything beyond the realm of mind, body, and senses where "I" cannot be in control is not real for fallen creation.

This is the eternal agenda of the Enemy—to kill personal identity, steal relationships, and destroy the dominion of God over humanity.

Fallen creation replaced God with the exclusive, sinful "I" of humanity. From a state of being that found fulfillment in and through God, working in and through our spirit, we moved to a state where "I" became the source of purpose and fulfillment in the mind and body. When God was removed,

He had to be replaced. The only two options were self and Satan. Both have proven disastrous in every generation.

Self became humanity's epicenter. While God can still be part of our language and agenda, self now reigns over Him. As long as we visit God on Sundays but let ourselves rule the other six days, as long as we worship God in church on Sundays but worship ourselves—along with our heroes in Hollywood, Silicon Valley, and Wall Street—the rest of the week, these are indicators of the fallen creation. The autonomy of the mind and body is a key indicator of the fallen creation.

KEY DEATH INDICATOR 9: THE POLITICS OF GOD AND MANKIND

Israel asked God for a king, but human government was not part of God's original design for humanity. When human beings lost the ability to commune with God and be governed by the supernatural law for which they were designed, lawlessness became the new dimension in which humanity found itself and became the norm. The abnormality of lawlessness became the new normal. God never intended Israel be ruled by kings, but in their fallen state, human beings desired to be ruled by other humans, so they created kings, queens, and political systems for governance.

I do not intend in any way to argue that government is bad or wrong. This system keeps the world not necessarily at peace, but in one piece. Human beings demanded this government, and God allowed it. Therefore, political systems are God-ordained, but they are subservient to His governance. We need to take note of how human political governance centers around the God theme. Experience in the present is an evidence of a historical truth.

There are five major political blocs:

1. The Communist bloc (no God)
2. The Hindu bloc (many gods)
3. The Buddhist bloc (God as a force)
4. The Islamic bloc (Allah as God)
5. The Christian bloc (one God)

There are no political systems in the world other than these five. There are no political blocs outside the concept of God. All are equal in their political incorrectness concerning Him. The politics of Christianity is the worst of all because we choose human governance rather than God's governance over human beings. We think a Christian president is the solution to the problems of the Western world. This illusion simply reflects our fallen nature.

Christians are called to pray for leaders and pay taxes, but if we think the answer to the nation's troubles lies in political governance, we have bought into a major deception of the Enemy. This was the lie that built the Soviet empire, Communist China, and the Islamic State. This is also the lie afflicting my home country of India and America. When any theism is used to govern human beings, rulers engage in the greatest abuse of power. Religious ideology defining political ideology that determines human behavior has been and is the historical curse of humanity.

Political systems cannot define human behavior irrespective of any religious influence they may have. When the laws of religious politics supersede the personal relationship with God, tyranny will rule. This will be the case whether a political system is labeled conservative Christian, liberal Christian, or anything in between—even if it uses the name of Jesus.

Twenty-first-century Christians have been deceived into thinking that conservative politics is Christlike. A conservative party is a political party and not a spiritual lifestyle. Christian identity cannot and should not be derived from a political ideology. Christian identity is a constant; Christian political ideologies are variables. As time, technology, and culture progress, Christian political ideologies will also change.

The kings and prophets in the Old Testament represented people before God. In the New Testament representing the New Covenant, there is one King and one kingdom. This is not about nations, but a personal relationship between God and individuals.

Just as the Israelites asked for a king so they could be like the nations around them, Western Christians are asking for a political system with Jesus as their King. God's response is the same as it was back then—there can be no national king, only a personal King.

We should most certainly have Christians in politics, but politics can never become Christian by nature. Throughout history, people have used the name of Jesus to gain political credibility, and disaster has always resulted. There have been many Christlike politicians but no Christlike political systems. From the time of Constantine, we have seen God become a national identity and not a personal identity. The deception of a national or political Christian identity is that having affiliation to the ideology keeps us from having a relationship with the Person. Having a relationship with a Christian political ideology is not the same as having a relationship with Jesus Christ.

Western Christians have been deceived into thinking that when Christians are in politics, politics is Christian. When Christians are in politics, Christianity has influence, but when politics becomes Christian, deception results. When politics becomes Christian, the law of Christian politics becomes the law of God. This failing reflects fallen creation.

This has happened in Soviet Russia, Islamic Iran, and Christian America. This is happening in Communist China and Buddhist Tibet. American Christians think the law of Christian America supersedes the law of God. No political ideology is the same as biblical Christianity. This blindness keeps people from questioning Christian political ideology and from comparing the law of God and the law of Christian politics. Conservative political ideology is not biblical Christianity.

Political systems were designed to govern the land and not to dictate spirituality. Biblically and historically, persecution has broken out when there is a contradiction between the law of God and the law of the land. There will be no persecution in America as we have seen in other religious political blocs, because the law of Christian political ideology will align itself with the desires of the culture for political gain. When this comes in the name of Christ, Christians will be deceived into following the political system, thinking it is Christian.

When Christians in America think Democratic or Republican political ideology is the same as biblical ideology, political ideology becomes truth. No one does a comparison to see if Christian political ideology is actually in line with biblical truths. When Soviet Russia outlawed Bibles, Bibles were smuggled into Russia. When the Supreme Court forbade Bibles in public schools, American Christians accepted this and changed their lifestyle to follow the law of the land. When communist China barred church gatherings, people continued to gather, were beaten, lost their jobs, and were thrown in jail. When the Supreme Court prohibited prayer in public schools, Christians stopped praying there. The law of God supersedes the law of the land in every political system except the Christian conservative political bloc.

We are spiraling downward, not because of any particular cultural issue, but because we have replaced the God of politics with the politics of God. Judgment will come because we have mistaken conservatism for Christlikeness. We have given priority to the Christian political system rather than Christ's governance of humanity. We have adjusted the law of God to suit human laws.

Just as Muslim radicals use Allah and the Qur'an to advance their political agenda, Western politicians use Jesus and the Bible to advance their agenda. Christians never have and never will need permission to express their Christian identity. A dove never asks permission to be kind and gentle, because those traits form its identity. One of the marks of the twenty-first-century religion called Christianity is that Christians ask political and legal permission to live out their Christian identity.

Should Christians fight for religious freedom? Absolutely, yes. Should Christians fight for freedom to live out their Christian identity? Absolutely not. There is no evidence anywhere in the Bible that the children of God followed the law of the land when it contradicted the law of God or that they asked permission of the government to live out the law of God. When parents in America advise their children to take their Bible to church but not to public school, they show themselves to be followers of twenty-first-century religion called Christianity, not biblical Christianity.

Finally, consider this. How does God's justice system work when Christians in northern India die for refusing to deny their Christian identity when it contradicts the law of the land, while Christians in America follow the law of the land and express their Christian identity only under the right circumstances? Indian Christians deny the law of the land and follow the law of God, while American Christians follow the law of the land, thinking this is not denying the law of God. Western Christians must realize that following the law of the land when it contradicts the law of God is a direct denial of His kingship. This is a symptom of Christian religion and not a sign of biblical Christianity. When our citizenship is in Heaven, we will follow the laws of God, for that is who we will become. The religion of

Christianity forces a caterpillar to act like a butterfly; a relationship with Christ transforms the caterpillar into a butterfly.

KEY DEATH INDICATOR 10: GOOD INTENT VS. GOD INTENT

Moses derived his personal identity from who he was told to be—a Hebrew child. His identity resulted in his actions. As we see throughout the book of Exodus, life did not always go the way Moses expected. He had to flee Egypt. His actions did not achieve his intended results. His people did not respond the way he expected. The "I" of Moses wanted to achieve things for God and fulfill His purpose. The result was forty years camping out in the desert! Fallen human beings can never accomplish God's purposes, however great their intentions might be. Good intent is not God intent.

Saul's plan to offer a sacrifice to God was extremely logical but unfortunately not very spiritual (1 Samuel 13). What is right in the mind is often not right in the spirit. Using the mind to follow the principles of the Spirit is religion. Allowing the Spirit to transform the mind, resulting in the transformed mind, enabled and empowered to follow the leading of the Spirit, is relationship. An untransformed mind can try to follow the principles of the Spirit, and that is when Christianity becomes deeply emotional, locational, circumstantial, and burdensome.

Fallen human beings:

+ Confuse good intent with obedience
+ Think that working for God is more important than obeying God
+ Believe that doing for God is more important than becoming like Jesus
+ Rationalize the things of God in the mind and body

KEY DEATH INDICATOR 11: DESIGNATED CHRISTIANITY

> Israel's watchmen are blind, they all lack knowledge; they are all mute dogs, they cannot bark; they lie around and dream, they love to sleep. They are dogs with mighty

appetites; they never have enough. They are shepherds who lack understanding; they all turn to their own way, they seek their own gain. "Come," each one cries, "let me get wine! Let us drink our fill of beer! And tomorrow will be like today, or even far better." (Isaiah 56:10–12)

Fallen human beings can be given the titles of shepherds or leaders yet still be spiritually blind and self-seeking. A spiritual enterprise being successfully run does not validate its spirituality. God is not necessarily at work just because thousands of people attend a church. The vast size of an audience does not validate the spiritual authenticity of the platform.

The word of the Lord came to me: "Son of man, prophesy against the shepherds of Israel; prophesy and say to them: 'This is what the Sovereign Lord says: Woe to you shepherds of Israel who only take care of yourselves! Should not shepherds take care of the flock? You eat the curds, clothe yourselves with the wool and slaughter the choice animals, but you do not take care of the flock.'" (Ezekiel 34:1–3)

This is what the Lord says: "As for the prophets who lead my people astray, they proclaim 'peace' if they have something to eat, but prepare to wage war against anyone who refuses to feed them." (Micah 3:5)

How can Ezekiel and Micah be asked to prophesy against the shepherds of Israel? The phrase "Woe to you shepherds!" is a paradox. The title does not necessarily reflect the quality of the individual. Fallen human beings can overlook quality and live by designations rather than the authenticity of a spiritual relationship.

God does not care about the spiritual titles people give themselves. Fallen human beings, even those with a prophetic designation, can act for their personal benefit and say what their listeners want to hear to gain financial profit. In fallen creation, designation and office supersede everything else.

> Her leaders judge for a bribe, her priests teach for a price,
> and her prophets tell fortunes for money. Yet they look for
> the Lord's support and say, "Is not the Lord among us? No
> disaster will come upon us." (Micah 3:11)

Jesus encountered this same religious system. The Person of God, for whom all religious ceremonies were created, came to earth and challenged the people. They thought they were running this religious system for God, but He placed it under His judgment.

God had told human beings to create the system according to His guidelines, but they left God out, operating the system for self-centered gain. Most Christian religious systems might be God-originated but are not God-sustained.

> Then Jesus said to the crowds and to his disciples: "The
> teachers of the law and the Pharisees sit in Moses' seat.
> So you must be careful to do everything they tell you. But
> do not do what they do, for they do not practice what they
> preach." (Matthew 23:1–3)

Jesus was warning His listeners when He says of the Pharisees, "Do not do what they do. Just do as they say." He was pointing out that what the Pharisees preach and what they do are opposites. It is not what we say, but who we are, that matters to Jesus.

Like many revival movements, the Pharisee sect among the Jews started with good intent. The name *Pharisees* in Hebrew means "separatists, or the separated ones." They were also known as *chasidim*, which means "loyal to God, or loved of God."

Fallen human beings can take all that God creates and make it all they want. Jesus recognized humanity's fallen identity in dealing with the Pharisees. We will convert God's spiritual system into a religious system of our own. Spiritual designations, accomplishments, and systems become monuments to human glory. We have perfected the art of making ourselves look good, defining our identity inside and outside the church by what we do, say, and possess, as well as by all that pleases the mind and body.

We must realize that Jesus was not talking to Roman soldiers but to religious leaders. The religious system was at the receiving end of His whip. We are capable of corrupting an incorruptible system, making the counterfeit look like the original.

Key Death Indicator 12: Celebrities of Religion

> Some time after this, Jesus crossed to the far shore of the Sea of Galilee (that is, the Sea of Tiberias), and a great crowd of people followed him because they saw the signs he had performed by healing the sick. ... After the people saw the sign Jesus performed, they began to say, "Surely this is the Prophet who is to come into the world." Jesus, knowing that they intended to come and make him king by force, withdrew again to a mountain by himself. ... Jesus answered, "Very truly I tell you, you are looking for me, not because you saw the signs I performed but because you ate the loaves and had your fill." (John 6:1–2, 14–15, 26)

Fallen humanity has the ability to find the supernatural in the natural. Jesus did not perform miracles to gain followers. His miracles were intended solely to point people to God in a dimension beyond the mind and body, but the nature of human beings is to point the miracles back to themselves.

We love creating celebrities. Facebook, Twitter, Instagram, and especially YouTube thrive on the celebrity system. Through our vast media, we have established a system to create celebrities and then worship them. We take normal human beings, label them as idols, put them on a pedestal, and when we grow tired of them, push them off. Then these people are left to figure out who they actually are.

We love to become idols, we love to create idols, and we love to see our idols fall. Then we can start the process all over again.

This can also be seen in our hormonal chemistry. Oxytocin is called the love hormone. Cortisol is called the stress hormone. When we have a Sunday morning high from church and a Monday morning low at work, these effects are invariably due to oxytocin and cortisol.

Fallen human beings can easily mistake the effects of oxytocin for spirituality. In situations when these levels are high, people will feel and behave spiritually. When circumstances change, hormonal levels drop off, and people return to their original fallen identity. Moving from high to low, they want the high again.

We go from one spiritual gathering to another, hoping to see an expression of God, not realizing that each expression is an invitation to experience Him. Frustration, disappointment, and hopelessness are growing inside and outside the church. Too many souls are disillusioned; too many of religion's celebrities are failing. The quality of character inside and outside the church is leveling off to become the norm. Christians are trying to defend a rapidly declining system. Religious celebrities are desperately trying to defend a losing institution.

Key Death Indicator 13: Fallen Freedom

> Before the coming of this faith, we were held in custody under the law, locked up until the faith that was to come would be revealed. (Galatians 3:23)

For the past several years, I have worked with inmates and their families to ensure that the children do not also end up in prison. Our goal is to break the generational recidivism that plagues the prison system in America. When I first stepped into a maximum-security facility, met the inmates, and spoke to them, I was hit by a chilling realization: I am like many of them. I am separated from these men by a very thin line, and many of them are where they are because of a momentary lack of self-control that brought harm to communities and innocent lives. Still, we are not that different.

I also realized that all of us are in a prison. Whether we are housed inside one or living on the outside, we all are locked up in our inner selves. All of us suffer regret, remorse, guilt, and bondage. Every emotion experienced in a jail cell resides inside each soul.

Fallen creation is like a prisoner serving a life sentence. When a person expects to spend the next several decades inside a cell, he or she finds a kind of freedom even in prison. The space inside becomes a version of liberty. There is no point in fighting it or feeling regret. Slowly, slavery becomes the new freedom. Eventually, the prisoner forgets what real freedom is, just as a slave can forget what freedom is. Far too many live today being slaves in their inner being, seeking for spiritual freedom, a spiritual freedom that is not about belief but experiencing spiritual liberty.

A PERFECT YET FLAWED DESIGN

A banana tree is planted perfectly in the soil. It grows for a couple of months, and suddenly the emerging leaves curl, resulting in a condition called bunchy top disease. This is but one example of nature's perfect creation gone wrong.

A virus infects a software program so it no longer functions as designed. Nuclear power can light up cities but also destroy human life. Every security system can be hacked. Every human creation has been destroyed or compromised, exposing a flawed design.

How can we explain why a teenager gets up one morning and shoots people at his school? Science keeps attributing such tragedies to chemical imbalances in the brain, and that is often correct, but we must go beyond the physical realm.

We can derive a deeper lesson from these occurrences. We must go back to the drawing board, look at the original design, and fix the fundamentals that caused the flaw. Every flaw has a root cause, and identifying this allows us to fix the design. We can find the cause for every flaw in the things we create, but we never look inward to understand that we ourselves are flawed and in need of a spiritual fix.

The thousands of people in misery in our prisons and addiction centers can be perfectly restored. Millions of people in our society appear perfect on the outside but are lonely, fearful, and desperately seeking love. All of this can change. But instead of demonstrating what love is, we fight over the design flaws in people. Instead of being loving, we force people into certain behaviors.

Many civilizations have produced rich literature on God and humanity. *Mahabharatha* and *Ramayana*, written hundreds of years before Christ, are all about the cosmic war within us. The Greeks and Romans wrote volumes about God and the human race. How much more evidence do we need for this singular hunger to reach out and bring the supernatural into the natural? People desperately desire supernatural communion.

When God became man, the announcement of His birth included the name Immanuel, which means "God with us." This does not mean God is simply *among* us. He is *with* us! *Us* in Greek is *ego*, which means "I" or "me." The incredible fix for the design flaw in human beings is revealed.

"God with us" must invade the "I."

Moving forward in these pages, you will walk into death. You will face the cross, where disruption begins. You will confront the paradox of death giving birth to life in the human spirit. The cross of Christ is a symbol of death and the gateway to experiencing life.

PART IV
NEW CREATION

This grace must give vent to itself and be manifested, for it is the very law of the divine nature, not merely *to be*—but to *manifest itself*. **This is the law of all being—to bring forth that which it contains**; in other words, to manifest *itself*; as in the case of the seed sown in the ground; a law which, in the creature, is the finite copy or image of that which has its seat and origin in the infinite Creator himself. The sun cannot but shine; the fountain cannot but pour forth its waters; the seed cannot but shoot up and bear fruit after its kind. Just so, divine goodness cannot but spread itself out, divine holiness cannot but come forth, divine wisdom cannot but give utterance to itself, and divine grace cannot but unfold its riches. —Horatius Bonar, 1867 (emphasis added)

> Now we look inside, and what we see is that anyone united with the Messiah gets a fresh start, is created new. The old life is gone; a new life burgeons! Look at it! All this comes from the God who settled the relationship between us and him, and then called us to settle our relationships with each other. God put the world square with himself through the Messiah, giving the world a fresh start by offering forgiveness of sins. (2 Corinthians 5:17–19 MSG)

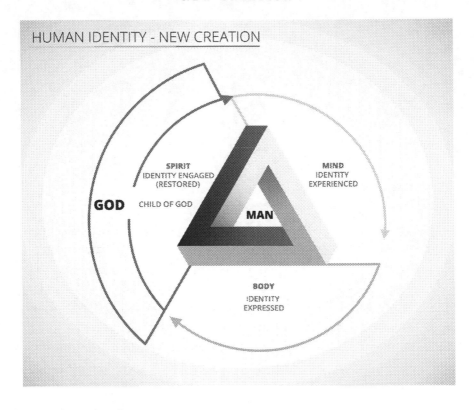

HUMAN IDENTITY - NEW CREATION

SPIRIT
IDENTITY ENGAGED
(RESTORED)

MIND
IDENTITY
EXPERIENCED

GOD   CHILD OF GOD

MAN

BODY
IDENTITY
EXPRESSED

The Purpose of Jesus and the Cross

The new creation takes humanity far beyond religious symbols, spiritual rituals, denominations, disciplines, and routines.

Jesus did *not* come to the earth to:

+ Replace Jewish customs with His customs
+ Replace Jewish rituals with His rituals
+ Replace Jewish religion with His religion
+ Replace going to a synagogue with going to a church
+ Whitewash the old
+ Refurbish humanity

Jesus came to the earth to:

- Replace the "opium of the people" with a relationship no high could offer
- Rebirth the human spirit to reconnect with the Spirit of God
- Establish an ongoing Spirit-to-spirit communication, communion, and companionship with God
- Transform the mind to be enabled to live from the divine nature and not from the old nature
- Birth a new transformational lifestyle of love and unity
- Build a new kingdom community
- Provide a new filter through which human beings could see themselves
- Provide a new filter through which human beings could see others
- Provide a new filter through which human beings could see the world
- Provide us with a new way to experience life lived in community

This lifestyle is based not simply on belief, but on the relational experience as a consequence of belief. This relational ongoing journey is true in any relationship. After a wedding, does a couple simply believe they are married and then meet for an hour once a week or do they begin to walk daily in communion, communication, and companionship resulting in doing life together?

Life disruption does not fix a broken system but creates a new system. Jesus, the Ultimate Life Disruptor, had arrived. He brought about a new creation by rewriting the story of life.

THE INVISIBLE IMPREGNATES THE VISIBLE: THE BIRTH OF CHRIST

A problem in the body requires a physical solution; in the mind, an intellectual and mental solution; in the spirit, a spiritual solution.

> This is how the birth of Jesus the Messiah came about: His mother Mary was pledged to be married to Joseph, but

before they came together, she was found to be pregnant
through the Holy Spirit. (Matthew 1:18)

Of the many obvious reasons for the virgin birth of Jesus, the one of
most profound importance is that man did not become God, define God,
or even find God, but God Himself took on human likeness.

+ The birth of Jesus was a dimension invasion.
+ The life of Jesus was a dimension revelation.
+ The death of Jesus was a dimension conquest.
+ The resurrection of Jesus was a dimension invitation.
+ The purpose of Jesus is to give spiritual life to a spiritually dead
  humanity.

But when the set time had fully come, God sent his Son,
born of a woman, born under the law, to redeem those
under the law, that we might receive adoption to sonship.
(Galatians 4:4–5)

The Spirit that created the human spirit and breathed life into human
beings became man to reanimate the human spirit. Christ was born as a
natural man to provide the way to be reborn in humanity. The objective
of Jesus' life, death, and resurrection was to restore humanity's original
identity. Salvation is not just about a place where we go after death but about
a Person with whom we relate when we are alive.

A womb in the spirit of every man and woman awaits impregnation
by the Spirit of God so each person can be born again. Everyone has this
potential for rebirth. Until God is born in a person, this spiritual womb is
inactive and waiting to be reborn. This is the deep yearning for something
more that all humanity experiences. As the womb of a woman has the
potential to produce physical life, there is potential for life in the spirit in
every human. Only a woman can experience the yearning to give birth in the
physical realm, but *all* of humanity yearns for rebirth in the spiritual realm.

The question of "Who am I?" is answered when the human spirit is
reborn in this spiritual womb. This womb cannot be impregnated by mere
human decision but only by the Spirit of God. Birth from a woman brings

human life. Being born of God brings about the new creation in man and woman, redefining and reforming personal identity. Being a child of God is an experience of identity in the spirit of humanity. And if physical birth is experientially real, then the spiritual rebirth is just as real. Flesh gives birth to flesh, while Spirit gives birth to spirit. From our identity being defined in the intellectual and physical, we experience spiritual identity through rebirth of the spirit and in relationship with God through the Spirit.

The birth of Jesus through Mary showed how the supernatural could pierce the natural. An angel announced the conception of Jesus. The invisible announced to the visible the birth of the invisible into the visible realm. The Holy Spirit conceived the inconceivable. The Unlimited One chose to be contained in a woman's womb by His own power. A perfect God brought the perfect solution to imperfect humanity, conceived in the imperfect human vessel, Mary. The birth, life, suffering, death, and resurrection of Jesus mirror the process of how humanity can experience spiritual rebirth that enables anyone to partake in the divine nature. The historical event of the invisible impregnating the visible can become a present reality.

PERSON BEFORE PERFORMANCE

As soon as Jesus was baptized, he went up out of the water. At that moment heaven was opened, and he saw the Spirit of God descending like a dove and alighting on him. And a voice from heaven said, "This is my Son, whom I love; with him I am well pleased" (Matthew 3:16–17).

The public introduction of Jesus began with a declaration of His identity by His Father. The personal identity of Jesus superseded His actions. The Person of Jesus was of greater importance than His performance, because His performance was simply an overflow of His Person. Before Jesus had ever performed any miracle or taught any truth, God said He was well pleased because of Jesus' position of Sonship. Jesus' actions sprang from who He was. They did not define His Sonship or His identity. The actions of Jesus did not define the identity of Jesus. The religion of Christianity defines identity by what we do, while the relationship that Jesus came to establish is for humanity to experience sonship identity and then to express it.

The Spirit of God descended on Jesus, and His true identity was revealed. God said, "This is my Son!" Heaven stood at attention. This is the greatest statement in human history. God the Father declared the identity of His Son through the Holy Spirit.

The spiritual dimension declared His Sonship identity. The mind heard and understood this identity as the Son of God and then was expressed through His body. There existed a perfect interdimensional interplay from the beginning of Jesus' life on earth. This was the standard operating procedure of God and remains the same today, as we experience our personal identity as children of God through the re-birthed dimension of our spirit. We understand this cognitively in our minds through transformation, and therefore express that identity through our bodies by living the moral and social compass of Jesus.

Christ knew who He was before He did anything as the Messiah. His external expression was an overflow of His perfect internal experience of communication, communion, and companionship with the Father. He experienced the Father before He expressed the Father. This differentiates the religion of Christianity from the relationship in Christianity.

The good news of Jesus Christ is about the ultimate love relationship where the supernatural filters into the natural so the natural can experience the supernatural. The singular Voice that can make human beings complete is the Father's. The one pronouncement that can fill the inner void is His declaration of "You are My child."

The realm of the spirit speaks, and then the realm of the mind understands the relationship and becomes transformed to become in sync with the spirit, and the realm of the body then expresses the relationship, operating seamlessly in Jesus with no compartmentalization. He lived *of* the Spirit, *by* the Spirit, and *through* the Spirit in perfect communion. The journey of Christianity enables us to be transformed to live as Jesus lived.

Christ's life was not about demonstrating how human beings *should* live but about how they *can* live. He came to show humanity the Source *from* which to live.

Because we are so performance-oriented today, we look at the life of Jesus primarily through the worldview of what He accomplished. But Jesus did not come to make bad-performing people into good performers. Jesus did not come simply to gain a following. His performance was a reflection of His identity as the Son of God.

He showed the world the perfect functioning of the supernatural realm of God, the supernatural realm in humanity, the human mind, and the human body, all in relationship to one another. Jesus showed humanity how the new creation lives from the spirit. How Jesus lived (cause) is foundational, and what He did (effect) is consequential. Christianity is not based on imitating Jesus' actions, but experiencing His methodology. *How* He lived is of far greater significance than *what* He did.

Supernatural Man: The Life of Jesus

The miracles of Jesus revealed the supernatural realm to humanity and showed the capability of the supernatural invading the natural. Miracles were not and are not an end; they have no meaning or value by themselves because every religion involves supernatural display. What happens *after* the miracle determines the *origin* of the miracle.

Does it create a relational intimacy that transforms mankind to the image and consequential lifestyle of Jesus? The New Testament is filled with accounts of miracles through which Jesus demonstrated that the spirit realm of God had the power to influence the spirit realm in humanity, resulting in a transformational experiential relationship with the Person of God.

The good, the bad, and the ugly of life's situations are invitations to look beyond the obvious picture in front of us. Both the beauty and destructive ability of nature are markers that direct us to also look beyond the obvious physical sight. All of life offers little clues throughout to go beyond the obvious of what anyone might see. The physical journey of life is an invitation to the spiritual journey of life.

From the time of the Israelites' exile to the arrival of Jesus, there were countless misperceptions about God. Religion was:

+ Location-centric. (People went to the temple.)
+ Racial. (People had to belong to the Jewish race.)

+ Denominational. (People had to be Pharisees or Sadducees.)
+ Behavior-centric. (People had to do certain things to please God.)

Jesus refocused humanity from the mind and body, from locations and denominations, from race and color to reconnecting the supernatural in human beings to the supernatural dimension of God.

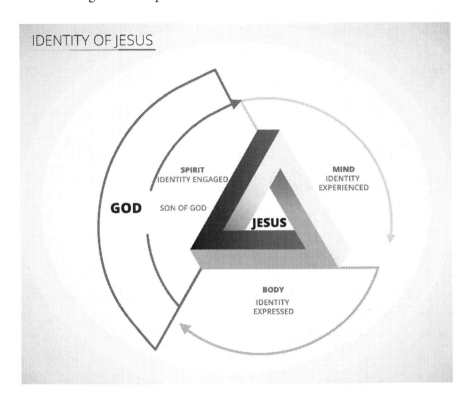

DIMENSION INTERCONNECTION

Eastern and Middle Eastern mysticism is predominantly about silencing the body to enter Nirvana, the state of perfection. People go to the Himalayas and into caves in the mountains, away from all physical distraction, to silence the triggers of the mind and body to experience spiritual bliss. Buddha said this is reached through the "Noble Eightfold Path." The other extreme is to use the mind to reach out to the supernatural, believing that what happens in the physical realm does not matter.

We are integrated beings with a dysfunctional spirit and fully functional mind and body. Jesus did not come to separate the human realms but to produce a new creation that lives in the physical realm through the power of the spiritual realm. Such is a consequence of the transformation of the mind by the supernatural. The new creation offers a new power source for humanity. The cross of Christ integrates the natural state of mankind supernaturally. The mind following spiritual rules is religion; the mind being transformed by the Spirit is relationship.

> When they came to Jesus, they found the man from whom the demons had gone out, sitting at Jesus' feet, dressed and in his right mind; and they were afraid. (Luke 8:35)

Jesus influenced the supernatural dimension in this man, causing demons to leave, restoring the man to his right mind. Grasping the implications of this miracle is important because Jesus showed that when demons were exposed in the realm of the human spirit, there were consequences in the realm of the mind and body. External change is a consequence of internal change. Jesus fixed the internal problem, so the external was resolved as a result.

The life of Jesus set the stage, created the precedent, and demonstrated how human beings could live in the new creation God would establish on earth. Our experience validates His teaching. The proof of the reality of Jesus is not just belief but our present spiritual transformation resulting in living out His way of life. Not by simply trying harder but by becoming more like Him. The lifestyle of Jesus had two components—internally of communion, communication, and companionship with the Father and externally of doing what He experienced internally. This internal spiritual relationship resulting in the external supernatural lifestyle is the true journey of Christianity.

HEAVEN'S SUPREME COURT

> God presented Christ as a sacrifice of atonement, through the shedding of his blood—to be received by faith. He

did this to demonstrate his righteousness, because in his forbearance he had left the sins committed beforehand unpunished—he did it to demonstrate his righteousness at the present time, so as to be just and the one who justifies those who have faith in Jesus. (Romans 3:25–26)

Even though we have a flawed operating system, an incredible sense of right and wrong is ingrained in us. We tend to judge even God Himself through this lens but we would be better off looking to His Supreme Court for our views on justice and judgment.

Sin that separated God and mankind had to be punished, so He took it upon Himself. The Judge who handed down the sentence then stepped down to take the punishment for the crime. The cross is where justice started and judgment ended. Twenty-first-century Christianity has made this truth such a theological theory that the awe of this present experiential reality in Christ's incredible sacrifice is all but lost on us.

When people step up through crowd-funding platforms to help others they do not know, we see the incredible beauty of humanity reaching out. We have lost a similar sense of awe of what Christ did on the cross because we have restricted it to a mystical theology and failed to see it as becoming a practical and personal biography. The cross is the expression of God's love, justice, mercy, and judgment. The objective of God's Supreme Court and of His judgment is to allow humanity to have a relationship with Him through a Spirit-to-spirit communion. The power of the cross is not in belief alone but in what happens when people believe.

This method of atonement—paying for sin—differs in world religions and in them all it is inconsequential in mankind for the present life. Going to the Himalayas, Ganges, Rome, Mecca, or other places for salvation have one common goal—Heaven after death. Religions of the world present a futuristic salvation based on a present event or actions of mankind. The cross of Christ offers a present relationship with God based on a historical event.

The disobedience of mankind in the garden caused him to lose his sonship. God paid the price in taking the punishment on Himself that was due to mankind. The Perfect took on the sin of the imperfect to make the imperfect perfect.

God had to be just in His demand and solution, so He became man to take the punishment for *all* humanity. Until the problem of sin was resolved, the relational problem between God and humanity could *not* be resolved. Mankind's state of being as cosmic orphans could only be changed when God had dealt with humanity's state of sin that separated mankind from Him. The cosmic vacuum could only be filled when the chasm that created the vacuum was filled. Human identity for the child of God could only be restored when the problem that destroyed that identity was resolved.

THE POWER OF SIN BROKEN

God made him who had no sin to be sin for us. (Romans 5:21)

The death he died, he died to sin once for all. (Romans 6:10)

But you know that he appeared so that he might take away our sins. And in him is no sin. (1 John 3:5)

Sin was born in the garden. Sin died on the cross. The power that created the cosmic vacuum separating humanity from God was destroyed there. When the price of sin was paid, the cross then bridged the chasm that separated mankind from God. There is now provision for the Spirit of God to rebirth and coexist in the human spirit; thereby, the cosmic vacuum that causes the mirage of life may come to an end. This *can* be experienced as a present reality!

When the crucified Jesus said, "It is finished," He ensured the full price had been paid for *all* sin for *all* humanity for *all* time (John 19:30). Because of this, the responsibility of mankind paying the price for sin ceased to exist forever. No earthly priest, pastor, imam, or guru is required as an intermediary between God and mankind because of Christ's work on the cross.

When the debt is paid in full, the power of the lender is broken. When the full price for the penalty of sin on behalf of mankind was paid on the cross, there was an incredible consequence that occurred in that the power as well as the state of sin was broken. The historical reality of the truth of the cross in achieving forgiveness for humanity becomes real when humanity lives in communion, communication, and companionship with God. The proof of a historical reality is its ability to transform into a present human experience. The evidence of the historical reality of the cross is its present ability to enable mankind to experience the identity of being a child of God.

> No one who is born of God will continue to sin, because God's seed remains in them; they cannot go on sinning, because they have been born of God. (1 John 3:9)

Saying we believe in the cross for forgiveness without experiencing the freedom of enslaving sin is a contradiction. The practicality of the cross is its capability to enable humanity to not do what it does not want to do. Sin is slavery. We are free to be delivered from *anything* that enslaves us. The cross empowers us to do what we want to do and not do what we do not want to do because the power of sin was and is broken there. This is true freedom!

Forgiveness Born

> In fact, the law requires that nearly everything be cleansed with blood, and without the shedding of blood there is no forgiveness. (Hebrews 9:22)

> In him we have redemption through his blood, the forgiveness of sins, in accordance with the riches of God's grace. (Ephesians 1:7)

> "Their sins and lawless acts I will remember no more." And where these have been forgiven, sacrifice for sin is no longer necessary. (Hebrews 10:17–18)

Jesus' sacrifice gave birth to forgiveness. His shed blood opened the door for the forgiveness of sin, allowing the new creation to be born. Humanity needs to experience forgiveness to extend forgiveness to one another. The reason we have so much hatred is because humanity does not experience forgiveness. Where forgiveness is not experienced, forgiveness cannot be extended. This is not a theological mystery but an experiential reality Jesus offers. For people to make claims about following Jesus and then to live in hatred and unforgiveness is a contradiction. *Experience* forgiveness; *extend* forgiveness.

While twenty-first-century Christians tend to rate sin from large to small, God never has. All sin is an equal state of rebellion against Him. The Enemy often fools us into thinking that a sin is too small to worry about or so big that the cross could never cover it. Let's be clear: the cross covers *all* sin in *every* person, because sin is not an act of doing but a state of being. The evidence of the historical reality of the cross is its present ability to enable mankind to experience the forgiveness of God!

One thing the world desperately needs today is a community of people who experience supernatural forgiveness so they can be natural in forgiving one another. Jesus came to create this community of people. When such a community calls itself a church but practices unforgiveness, this is the religion called Christianity. When individuals call themselves Christians and live a lifestyle of unforgiveness, they belong to this religion called Christianity.

THE POWER OF THE ENEMY IS BROKEN: THE RESURRECTION OF JESUS

The cross not only meets the legal obligation before God and solves the problem of sin in humanity but also destroys the power of the Enemy. Jesus rendered the Enemy powerless.

> Since the children have flesh and blood, he too shared in their humanity so that by his death he might break the power of him who holds the power of death—that is, the devil. (Hebrews 2:14)

> The reason the Son of God appeared was to destroy the devil's work. (1 John 3:8)

> And having disarmed the powers and authorities, he made
> a public spectacle of them, triumphing over them by the
> cross. (Colossians 2:15)

The stranglehold of humanity's enemy is broken. This is not a theological statement or Christian ideology. If Jesus' death on the cross is truth to be experienced, then the destruction of the Enemy's power is also truth to be experienced. The Devil can no longer hold humanity under his authority. Human beings have the choice to walk away from the control and slavery of Satan.

You and I did not have a choice when Adam chose to listen to the Enemy and, consequentially, became his slave. But today, you and I have the choice to walk away from this slavery of the cosmic vacuum in which the Enemy has placed us. The evidence of the historical reality of the cross is its present ability to enable mankind to experience freedom from the Enemy. We can choose to walk away in freedom—now.

Consider these vital statements about the disruption of the cross:

- The price for sin is paid by the sacrificial death of Jesus on the cross.
- The power of sin is broken by the sacrificial death of Jesus on the cross.
- The forgiveness of sin is achieved by the sacrificial death of Jesus on the cross.
- The righteousness of Jesus has met the righteous requirements of God for a rebirth of the human spirit.
- The Spirit of God can take residence in human beings and begin a spiritual relationship with the Father.
- All this occurred historically so it can become a present experiential reality.

A historical event took place in the natural that had supernatural implications, leading to a spiritual solution that humanity can choose to experience at any moment of time.

PHILOSOPHY BECOMES BIOGRAPHY: MANKIND EXPERIENCING GOD

This spiritual transaction is not just a legal supernatural accomplishment but also a functional completion. The proof that the judge has declared the guilty innocent becomes a reality when the convict walks free. Human spiritual identity is reborn to be experienced when people are pronounced innocent and become children of God. Freedom from spiritual captivity is proof of forgiveness and the pronouncement of innocence. The judgment has been rendered. The gates have been opened. The veil separating God and humanity has been torn down. The amazing truth of Christianity is that people may become new creations. God's side of the deal is done.

> But the people's minds were hardened, and to this day whenever the old covenant is being read, the same veil covers their minds so they cannot understand the truth. And this veil can be removed only by believing in Christ. Yes, even today when they read Moses' writings, their hearts are covered with that veil, and they do not understand. But whenever someone turns to the Lord, the veil is taken away. (2 Corinthians 3:14–16 NLT)

The twenty-first-century church is filled with people who believe that giving mental assent to this truth is enough. Believing that the veil has been taken away is totally different from experiencing life with the veil taken away! Their brand of Christianity consists of convincing others of what Jesus did. But a person may have a doctorate in theology and be able to explain all the details of what Jesus accomplished on the cross, yet still not personally hold the eternal life of God. Knowing the meaning and purpose of atonement, justification, reconciliation, and redemption does not guarantee a person has Jesus living inside. This happens only one way—through an experiential relationship with the Person of Christ. Removing the veil that separates humanity from God is not a confident declaration but a practical experience.

Twenty-first-century Pharisees justify belief alone as the singular passport to salvation and Heaven. This is like saying you plant the seed and then you can pick fruit. The seed can rot and die. The seed can be eaten away. The seed can be choked out. What happens after the seed is sown is what determines fruiting and harvest. What happens after the seed is sown is what determines if the seed has life or not. Disconnecting the seed from the fruit is one of the biggest heresies of the twenty-first-century religion called Christianity.

A seed with life in it will germinate, grow roots, and form a shoot. It will fight diseases and drought, eventually bearing fruit when connected to the Source. When we believe in the cross of Christ, we will grow in a relationship with Him and will live out His lifestyle. When there is no life, there is no growth. This is *the* principle of life. When there is life, there is growth! The proof of our living is not our historical birthday, but the present ongoing growth that transforms us from two-cell human beings into maturity.

An authentic relationship with Jesus can be understood when we know the difference between evidence and expression. Expressions are not the primary evidence of living life. The *evidence* of a living plant is the active diffusion and osmosis occurring in the root system. The *expression* is the stem, branches, leaf, flower, and fruit. A dead plant is one where active diffusion in the roots stops permanently. The cause that enables life is evidence; the effect that life produces is expression.

The *evidence* of human life is the exchange of oxygen and carbon dioxide in the lungs and the beating heart. The *expression* of human life is our activities and what others see. A person is not pronounced dead when movement ceases, but when the exchange of air in the lungs stops and the heart quits pumping blood.

We cannot fake the evidence of life, but we have a unique ability to falsify our expressions. We cannot express life when our lungs stop functioning, but we can express happiness when we are suffering in sorrow. We can fake who we are by what we do.

An apple tree can produce only apples. A lion will not meow but roar. Identity and its corresponding expressions are synchronous in all of creation. But human beings have the ability to be one person on the inside and another on the outside.

Religion fixes expressions. Relationship fixes evidence.

Religion fixes behavior. Relationship allows life to be reborn, therefore changing behavior.

If we plant what we believe to be an apple tree but lemons appear, there is no way we can fix the fruit. The only response is to change the tree. Religion tries to rework the fruit, while relationship gives birth to a new tree.

Jesus came to plant a new seed and grow a new tree. The seed is the Word of God. The tree is the new creation formed in the individual. The fruit is the lifestyle of love, unity, and wholeness. Jesus came to create a new dimension in humanity that can commune with God and be cognitively experienced through transformation of the mind, therefore externally expressed. Jesus came to enable the mind not to be controlled by the old nature but to be in alignment with the Spirit of God. Jesus came to reset the origin of life in humanity. This is the evidence of life in Christianity—Spirit-to-spirit communion, communication, and companionship with God.

The cross enables humanity to experience this adoption—a private and personal journey of partaking in the divine nature of God Himself. Such is the evidence of life in Christianity.

The encounter between the newly born realm of the human spirit and the Spirit of God in a person is like the exchange of air inside the lungs. This is where the cosmic vacuum is filled. This is where the child cries out, "Abba Father." The Spirit of God and the mind of mankind begin the journey of an incredible interplay.

We experience our identity as children of God in the mind as a cognitive awareness of the spiritual Father-child relationship. This exchange between God and a human being takes place irrespective of situations, moods, and emotions. This supersedes everything in the mind and body. We all crave, work toward, and hope for this divine exchange that empowers our minds to experience God Himself. Then we will not need sinful acts to fill the inner emptiness in the midst of external success. Then we will not need to drown ourselves in alcohol because we do not have what we want. We journey in this incredible spiritual relationship, where the internal constant defines all external variables. This divine exchange enables the body to experience the explosive resurrection power of God, overcome the old nature, and overflow with external expression, not requiring special circumstances, locations, or permissions.

This incredible relational journey of inner spiritual intimacy between God and mankind is called Christianity. The more we are transformed to experience the internal evidence, the more external expression overflows. The evidence of salvation is this journey of transformation, where we cognitively recognize and become aware of God, leading to communion, communication, and companionship with God. If there is no transformation, there is no salvation. Transformation is not a destination but a journey. You can know you have reached the destination of salvation when you realize you are on the journey of transformation. There is nothing that is achieved in the realm of the mind and body that can compare to this incredible personal intimacy of love that humanity can experience on a constant and consistent basis.

My Own Struggle

What Jesus did for us by what He accomplished on the cross are incredible truths evidenced, experienced, and expressed by every generation since the first century. There was a season in my life when I did not believe this. Then there was a period when I did believe it. My greatest struggle was to bridge the gap between what I believed, what I experienced on the inside, and who I portrayed myself to be on the outside. I knew the truth of the cross, acknowledged the truth, and understood the truth. I comprehended all that Jesus had done on my behalf. I expressed all that I was supposed to do. But I had not experienced what Jesus could do *in* me. The greatest tragedy was to have confused what Jesus did on my behalf for what Jesus would accomplish in me on an ongoing basis of relational love. I thought simply believing in the theory was experiencing the theory.

Was I supposed to believe in what Jesus accomplished on the cross, or was I supposed to experience the consequence of that work in me?

Was I supposed to believe in the peace of God, or was I supposed to experience the God of peace?

When Jesus said He would never leave me nor forsake me, was I to believe it or was I to experience it? Am I to believe He is with me, or am I to experience His being with me?

Was I supposed to believe in the love of God, or was I supposed to experience the God of love? Is peace and love what I believe, or are they what I experience? Or am I to just believe that I will experience them?

Was I supposed to believe that sin and the Enemy had been disarmed, or was I supposed to experience this reality through my ability to live a life that reflected Jesus?

Was the cross a statement of belief, or was it a place for giving birth to a relationship?

Was I to believe in the relationship the cross makes possible, or was I to experience the relationship?

While these questions might appear to be only semantics, these are very critical and crucial differences.

I accepted what Jesus did on my behalf. I touted what Jesus could do *through* me. But I struggled with what Jesus could do *in* me. My spirituality was circumstantial and locational. My belief and my behavior were in alignment, but I was still empty and swinging from spiritual highs to sinful self-destruction. I understood God's truths and tried to obey His rules in order to transform my behavior. I was desperately trying to fix the expressions, thinking it was *my* responsibility to change my behavior. Christianity became a burden and a load that I no longer wanted to carry. I had enough problems in my mind and body without adding another burden from another dimension!

The Bible gave me knowledge to talk about and even preach about God, but this did not transform me. For many years I sought this "spiritual experience" every week at church. I would sing and worship my heart out with great emotion. And I loved it. But through the weekdays, the emotion wore off and my inner reality burst forth with a vengeance. I thought this Jesus stuff was all belief and had no present relevance until my inner hunger for reality drove me to look at the Christian Scripture—the Bible—in a completely new way.

So I put aside all of my preconceived ideas about God, Jesus, the Holy Spirit, and the Bible so I could read its pages for what it is. I dropped all my denominational, geographic, cultural, and racial filters and read God's Word with fresh eyes, for what it is and not what I was thought it was *supposed* to be.

I began to realize:

- The Christian experience is fundamentally not emotional but spiritually transforming; not about how I feel but about into whom I am being transformed.
- The greatest spiritual experience is to be transformed into the image of Jesus, cognitively recognizing His reality in me, letting Jesus live His lifestyle through me.
- This is a journey of love between a Father and His child.
- Circumstances and location do not define this relationship.
- Emotions, music, and intonation of voice have nothing to do with the relationship of love Jesus came to establish.
- When I experience character transformation, the byproduct is an inner awareness of God.
- When I experience the transformation of my mind to the mind of Christ, an incredible inner testimony of the Spirit of God affirms I am a child of God.
- This is the identity of adoption we so long for in the deepest core of our inner being.

The Bible consistently compares the relationship between Christ and His children to a marriage, as in Ephesians 5:25 where Paul states, "Husbands, love your wives, even as Christ also loved the church, and gave himself for it."

Marriage begins with a beautiful event called a wedding that soon becomes a historical fact. That's why we take pictures and video. To describe marriage as an event of the past shows an incorrect understanding of this covenant between a man and woman. The event of a wedding gives birth to an incredible relationship of love between two people. While both have their good and bad qualities, they begin a lifelong journey of knowing one another, loving one another, and living for one another. Being with one another takes precedence over doing things for one another.

Marriage is between two imperfect people, while the relationship between God and a human being involves a Perfect and an imperfect person, with the Perfect making the imperfect perfect in this journey called life. Being with the Perfect is what we all long for. Being with Jesus is what we all desperately need. His disciples experienced and enjoyed Him physically when He was on the earth. The disciples of Jesus continue to experience and enjoy Jesus spiritually, even today.

There is a spiritual relationship that happens 24/7 and fills the cosmic vacuum in mankind. The mirage of life ends here. The purpose of mankind becomes the Person in mankind, and there is nothing greater than experiencing God as a cognitive constant as a consequence of transformation. The foundational game-changer of Christianity is all of mankind, being and becoming aware of the I Am of God that becomes the chief end of mankind, to experientially know God and enjoy Him while here on earth. The journey of a relationship with Christ is the destination of Christianity.

The Three M's:
Metric, Methodology, and Measurement

Knowledge of God's truth brings the freedom of God's Spirit that enables us to experience God's Person. We must transition from religious expressions being our evidence of spirituality to transformational spiritual communion becoming our evidence. This is the cognitive communion with God as a consequence of transformation of the mind by the Word of God.

We must make the transition from behavior based on knowledge to that which flows from spiritual transformation. Transitioning from expressions *becoming* my evidence to expressions *birthing* from my evidence is liberating. Christianity brings total freedom because what we do comes out of an overflow from whom we are transformed into. Actions are birthed from a transformed inner nature. When we become like Christ, we will behave like Christ.

Understanding metrics, methodology, and measurement in the new creation is crucial to experiencing the disruption of life. The theory of Christianity becomes a personal biography when we understand and apply these 3 M's of the new creation.

Metric is an outcome.

Methodology is the process used to achieve an outcome.

Measurement shows the progress of the methodology in achieving the metric.

Metric is the effect.

Methodology is the cause.

Measurement shows if the cause is creating the effect.

Metric, within the context of this book, is who we become and consequently what we experience.

Methodology is *how* we become spiritual, what God does, and what we do to experience the metrics.

Measurement is *whether* we are becoming spiritual and how we know for certain we are on the transformational journey.

Education has been a prime focus in raising my two children. Grades are the metrics, test results are the measurements, and studying is the methodology. If I want my son to get an A in calculus, I can emphasize the metric to him over and over again. My son can fast and pray to get an A. I can promise him rewards or threaten punishment to try to achieve the metric. He can be committed to getting an A, attend school regularly, and remain well behaved. He can believe he is capable of getting an A and tell the world how awesome an A would be, but none of this will get him an A.

When the measurement is done and grades are released, if all he has done is to believe, hope, and be committed to attending school, his metric will likely be an F.

My son will tell me how unfair it is that he did not make the grade after doing so many things right. I will respond by asking him, "Did you do what your teacher told you to do—study and complete all the exercises in the calculus textbook? Did you work on the methodology?"

The methodology to get an A in calculus is simple: study to understand the calculus book every day. When we follow the methodology of learning, we will achieve the metrics of good grades. Methodology is what we do; metrics are not. If we fully commit to the process, the results follow. To change the metric or outcome of grades, we must focus on the methodology of systematic learning. When we work on the methodology, the outcome changes. Work on the cause, and the effect changes.

I am a trained agriculturist. I know that to germinate a plant, I do not pull out the root or the shoot from the seed. All I do is pour water and give the plant proper nutrients, and the root and the shoot appear in due time. Germination and growth are metrics of the plant, while pouring water is the methodology.

We cannot force fruit from a plant, because fruit is a metric, an outcome. As we apply the methods of plowing, seeding, irrigation, and fertilizing, the fruit will come as a result. The plant does not will itself to produce fruit. To improve the production of fruit, we change the methodology, and, thereby, the outcome changes. There is a clear cause-and-effect principle at work.

As a businessman, I look at metrics such as sales performance. To improve this metric, some managers will shout at their salespeople, demanding better performance. They use incentives and disincentives to improve sales, looking solely at results and performance when all they care about is increased sales.

But effective sales managers know that sales numbers are only a metric, an indicator of an outcome. There is no point in focusing on the metric. So successful managers target the sales process or the methodology to achieve performance goals. They zero in on improving the effectiveness of salespeople. When they are transformed to become great at sales, the result is great sales performance. Change the methodology and you affect the results.

When we use the word *experience* in the context of this book, as well as in biblical Christianity, it is not emotional, not circumstantial, not locational but the:

- Spirit testifying to our spirit that we are children of God
- Individuals partaking in the divine nature of God
- Awareness of the body of the individual becoming the temple of God
- Inner constant that defines all external variables
- Inner compass that drives all human relationships

Understanding metrics, methodology, and measurement in the Bible while recognizing cause and effect in the experience of a relationship with Jesus Christ was the game-changer in my spiritual journey.

Key Life Indicators (Metrics) of the New Creation

In the previous section, we walked through the Key Death Indicators, or KDIs. Here, we will look at the Key Life Indicators, or KLIs, of the new creation that are the metrics we would experience as a consequence of the transformational relationship of communion, communication, and companionship with God.

KLIs are not what we do but who we become. They are not the causes of what we do but the effects or outcomes we will experience. We must remember that God produces these outcomes in us through transformation. The methodology section will outline how this transformation happens, but we must know the metrics before we learn the methodology. Understanding that these are results we will experience is foundational.

Key Life Indicator 1:
Filling the Cosmic Vacuum—
Outcomes in the Spirit Realm

Experiencing the New Dimension

When you were dead in your sins and in the uncircumcision of your flesh, God made you alive with Christ. (Colossians 2:13)

When a sperm and an egg come together, physical life is birthed. When the Spirit of God and the spirit of mankind come together, spiritual life is birthed. In Christ, we are made alive and given new life. This is not just what we confidently proclaim to believe, but what happens *when* we believe and what we will subsequently experience through transformation. This new life is an act and action of God in mankind, the game-changer of the cross of Christ.

In the above verse, Paul is not telling his audience to believe that they were made alive, but rather making a statement of fact that has happened in his audience. Our spirit—born dead—is now made alive and has the ability to commune with God, have a relationship with Him, listen to Him, and experience Him, all accomplished by God in us when we believe. Similar to the mind and body, there is a new dimension that is reborn in us which can consequentially be cognitively known by the mind and experienced by the body. There is a literal cohabitation of God in us. We can experience this objective reality in the subjective dimension. The evidence of conception is impossible to be concealed. The evidence of spiritual re-birth is impossible to be concealed. You will know it and the world will see it.

EXPERIENCING OUR IDENTITY: CHILD OF GOD

> The Spirit you received does not make you slaves, so that you live in fear again; rather, the Spirit you received brought about your adoption to sonship. And by him we cry, "Abba, Father." (Romans 8:15)

> See what great love the Father has lavished on us, that we should be called children of God! And that is what we are! (1 John 3:1)

When a mother gives birth to a baby, there is a relational identity established between the parent and child. Father-child and mother-child are the relational identities the baby experiences. The child does not believe these identities but experiences them. When we receive the Spirit of God in the new creation, He produces something that did not exist before. From slaves to sonship through adoption, knowing this metric is foundational to experiencing this new identity and is also the most powerful differentiator of biblical Christianity from religion. There is a spiritual identity conversion that happens in the human spirit by the Holy Spirit. As we journey this relationship of love with the Father, there is an inner awareness of adoption. This will bring a supernatural inner rest that we can experience in the midst of external unrest. It is this inner awareness of son and daughter identity that we all long for.

This identity change is not about:

+ Religion
+ Identification
+ Denomination
+ Sexual identity
+ Skin color

This identity change goes beyond the body and mind to the very core of who we are in our spiritual dimension. We become children of God—literally!

The death, burial, and resurrection of Jesus set Christianity apart from all other religions and allowed human beings to move from slaves to becoming sons and daughters who may now experience communion, communication, and companionship with their Father. This reality happens first in the human spirit, and is experienced through transformation in the mind and expressed through the body.

Adoption establishes God as our Father. Transformation enables us to experience God as our Father. Adoption and transformation results in us expressing the qualities of our Father to the world.

Here we find the transforming power of God. Whether our earthly fathers were present, absent, or abusive, God says that when we receive His Spirit, He takes residence in us, establishing a relationship by His Spirit, and that we may call Him "Abba Father." This is the disruption of the cross of Christ. The Spirit of God neutralizes every human experience and gives birth to a relationship that enables us to call out to Him as Father because we experience Him as Father.

> The Spirit himself testifies with our spirit that we are
> God's children. (Romans 8:16)

The word *testifies* in Greek is *symmartyreo*, a combination of two words—*sym*, a preposition denoting union, and *martyreo*, a verb derived from *martys*, which means a witness, someone who has personally experienced or seen something. An incredibly significant experiential outcome in Christianity is God's Spirit bearing witness to the human spirit that we are the children of God.

Despite great intellectual and physical achievements, human beings still desire this divine inner witness. We crave adoption as children of God through His Spirit. We hunger for this most intimate relationship. The cosmic vacuum is filled when the human mind recognizes the adoption of sonship. The inner longing for something more comes to an end when we experience Spirit-to-spirit communion of intimacy.

No matter how busy we may become in Christianity, Hinduism, Islam, atheism, communism, or any other "ism," we will continue to search until we discover the experience of God's adoption. Jesus paid the price for the eternal life of God to take up residence in human beings so He can do life together with us as Father and child. The greatest of all miracles happens when people experience the move from being cosmic orphans to being adopted into the family of God. There alone will we find rest for our spirit, mind, and body.

You can understand the effects of the wind but cannot fully grasp it until you feel the wind blow for yourself. Have you ever tried explaining to someone about an exciting experience and walked away thinking *my words did not at all adequately communicate what I know inside?* Have you ever thrown up your hands and exclaimed, "You just have to experience it for yourself!" The Father-child relationship is the ultimate example of the kind of experience the cross of Christ births in mankind.

The human mind recognizes and experiences the original design of connection to God. The evidence of the Christian faith is experiencing this communion between the Spirit of God and the reborn human spirit. This communion says, "Welcome home!" Like experiencing air, we cannot see it but we know it is there. An inner awareness of God is created in mankind resulting in the removal of the cosmic vacuum. There is nothing that humanity can do in and of itself in any dimension that can remove this void—that can end the mirage of life. Being a child of God is an experiential outcome in humanity that comes as a consequence of the supernatural adoption.

CREDIT OF RIGHTEOUSNESS: FREEDOM FROM GUILT AND FEAR

But now apart from the law the righteousness of God has been made known, to which the Law and the Prophets testify. This righteousness is given through faith in Jesus Christ to all who believe. (Romans 3:21–22)

The words "it was credited to him" were written not for him alone, but also for us, to whom God will credit righteousness—for us who believe in him who raised Jesus our Lord from the dead. (Romans 4:23–24)

We live in a world where regret, guilt, and self-condemnation rule, tormenting us and driving us to do things that keep us in perpetual inner suffering and pain. Physical pain is terrible; emotional pain is ruthless. But God credits righteousness in us by and through the cross of Christ. This righteousness is not the outcome of what we do, but something we receive and therefore experience. Righteousness is not what we earn but what is credited to us as a free gift because of Christ.

Imagine being in debt far beyond what you could possibly repay in your lifetime. Then someone comes along and tells you he is crediting your account to clear your debt and there is no need to repay. But believing yourself to be out of debt is not the same as experiencing financial freedom. Only people deep in debt can understand the difference between a promise and experience, between belief and freedom. The good news of the gospel is to cognitively experience the righteousness that is *given* to those who believe.

We do not need to go to Mecca, the Ganges River, a church, or to a priest or pastor for our righteousness, because the Creator credits us His righteousness so we can experience freedom from the debt of sin, guilt, and shame. This is one of the most incredible metrics we can experience in the new creation—an inner freedom that delivers us from all condemnation. Irrespective of what we have done in the past, we can have a new present, an incredible tomorrow, and an amazing future!

> Since the children have flesh and blood, he too shared
> in their humanity so that by his death he might break
> the power of him who holds the power of death—that is,
> the devil—and free those who all their lives were held in
> slavery by their fear of death. (Hebrews 2:14–15)

Our fears can be real or fabricated, due to our own mistakes or due to others' mistakes. But the greatest fear of all is the fear of death—the death of expectations, hope, the future, love, and life itself! The cross—the place of death for Jesus—is where the source of death was defeated, offering freedom from *all* fear. We do not simply believe we are free from fear but we are now made free. When God takes up residence in the human spirit, the fear of fear ends. This is an outcome to experience. This is a state of being and not a state of doing. This is the new creation and not just an upgrade in status from the fallen creation. Metrics are not what we believe but the outcomes we experience.

INTERPLAY OF SPIRIT, MIND, AND BODY

Without the interplay of spirit, mind, and body, we cannot cognitively know or experience the reality of what happens in our adoption as children of God. The reality of the metrics that happen in the human spirit must be filtered through the mind. Without this, Christianity remains only a religion. Christian experience occurs when reality of the spirit filters into the mind and is consequentially expressed through the body. There is total integration of the spirit, mind, and body in human beings.

Every metric the cross achieves in the realm of the spirit must enter the realm of the mind for human beings to experience God. This is the miracle of biblical Christianity. Knowledge and acceptance of the truth of the cross in the mind sets in motion consequences of the metrics becoming real in the spirit. The reality of these consequences connects back to the mind. We know the truth in the mind, triggering the rebirth of the spirit and the cohabitation of the Spirit of God. From then on, there is an ongoing journey of the Spirit influencing the mind, transforming our mind to the mind of Christ, so we become like Jesus. Consequentially, we experience the identity of being a child of God and all of its implications in the body.

A conscious decision in the mind results in an unconscious effect in the spirit, resulting in the conscious transformation of the mind by the Spirit to make conscious the reality of the Spirit in the mind.

Religion understands the truth and then tries to make behaviors happen through the mind. Relationship understands the truth and then allows the spirit to transform the mind, giving birth to metrics of the new creation in the mind and body. This is not mere semantics but the difference between twenty-first-century Christianity and the disruption of life that the cross of Christ brings to humanity.

We tend to forget Jesus Christ had a physical body with a brain. He is the ultimate example of how spirit, mind, and body interconnect to reveal the experiential reality of God. Jesus' life was not marred by sin. He did not operate from cache memory in relation to God or from knowledge about

God, nor was He independent of His Father even though He was the Son of God. The Spirit of God connected to the mind and body of Jesus had an incredible synchronous relationship. The journey of Christianity is humanity growing into and experiencing this spiritual communion and awareness.

> Jesus gave them this answer: "Very truly I tell you, the Son can do nothing by himself; he can do only what he sees his Father doing, because whatever the Father does the Son also does. For the Father loves the Son and shows him all he does. Yes, and he will show him even greater works than these, so that you will be amazed." (John 5:19–20)

> Don't you believe that I am in the Father, and that the Father is in me? The words I say to you I do not speak on my own authority. Rather, it is the Father, living in me, who is doing his work. (John 14:10)

> I am the vine; you are the branches. If you remain in me and I in you, you will bear much fruit; apart from me you can do nothing. (John 15:5)

Understanding how Jesus functioned is critical to understanding how He says we will function in the new creation. His mind was a fulcrum that could tap into, recognize, and interpret information from the spiritual realm and communicate this through the body. The new creation in humanity sets us up to operate as Jesus did and as we were originally designed.

KEY LIFE INDICATOR 2:
FUNCTIONAL INDICATORS—OUTCOMES
IN THE REALM OF THE MIND

THINKING METRICS

New behavior does not produce new thinking; new thinking produces new behavior because all actions begin as thoughts.

A new spirit leads to a new mind. We can apply the knowledge of scientific research and discovery to objectively know that the transformation of the mind does have a scientific basis. For example, brain plasticity, brain mapping, and cognitive neuroscience have offered amazing insight into the connection between the brain and behavior. The fMRI can measure specific areas of brain activity as an individual performs cognitive and motor tasks. Through these and other methodologies in the last few decades, science has discovered the brain can remap itself throughout a person's life.

For many years, scientists believed that the physical structure of the brain remained permanent. But modern science has discovered that the brain develops new neural pathways and alters existing ones to adapt to new experiences, always learning and creating new memories. In short, the brain can rewire itself.

While science is never a good starting point for the proof of God, the best evidence is a Spirit-rewired brain that experiences cognitive intimacy with God and lives out the lifestyle of Jesus. It is awesome when historians and scientists find information that confirms what God has said all along, but of greater importance is the evidence of transformed thinking that the Spirit of God develops in mankind.

How in the world could Stephen be compassionate towards the people who were stoning him to death (Acts 7)? He was expressing who he had become. How could Paul and Silas possibly sing hymns of praise in a dark and damp cell, shackled in chains (Acts 16:23–25)? No one told them to rejoice in times of suffering. What we read in the Scriptures is what they experienced. This was not some instruction they followed, but an experience they expressed. Thinking in alignment with the original design is an incredible outcome of belief. When there is no transformational thinking, such a belief is religion, even if that belief claims to be in Jesus Christ.

Sin Metrics

What shall we say, then? Shall we go on sinning so that grace may increase? By no means! We are those who have *died to sin*; how can we live in it any longer? Or don't you know that all of us who were baptized into Christ Jesus

were baptized into his death? We were therefore buried
with him through baptism into death in order that, just as
Christ was raised from the dead through the glory of the
Father, we too may live a new life. (Romans 6:1–4)

Being dead to sin is an incredible experiential outcome that the cross of
Christ produces in human beings. Religion teaches us to either fight sin
with our own willpower or enjoy sin because we know the love and grace of
God covers it all. One approach is legalism and the other is heresy.

The cross of Christ put sin to death so we may die to it and its power over
us may be destroyed. But we do not see sin as a metric, an outcome, or even
an effect because we have been taught to see sin as a cause. Disobedience
was the cause; the state of sin was the effect. When we see sin as an effect,
we realize that when the cause of sin is eliminated, the effect of sin is taken
care of as well. Freedom from things that enslave us that bring guilt and
condemnation is not what we believe, but an outcome we experience.

Everyone who sins breaks the law; in fact, sin is
lawlessness. But you know that he appeared so that he
might take away our sins. And in him is no sin. No one
who lives in him keeps on sinning. No one who continues
to sin has either seen him or known him. (1 John 3:4–6)

John is not talking about a methodology but a metric. He is outlining
an outcome of the cross. We can choose not to continue to sin, because
Jesus has taken care of it on the cross. Sin's power has been broken, and we
no longer need to obey the triggers it creates. We are free to not choose the
wrong things we no longer want to do and choose to do the right we are
transformed to do. This is true freedom. This is an incredible consequence
of the transformation of the mind, to no longer make choices that lead to
slavery and guilt. The new creation puts us in the state where we experience
freedom as a metric, an outcome, and an effect. Those who live in Him are
not those who do *not* sin but those who won't *keep* sinning.

From a lifestyle of sin, we progressively are transformed into a lifestyle
of freedom from sin and a lifestyle of love and unity.

KEY LIFE INDICATOR 3:
QUALITY INDICATORS—OUTCOMES IN
THE REALM OF THE BODY

> For this very reason, make every effort to add to your faith goodness; and to goodness, knowledge; and to knowledge, self-control; and to self-control, perseverance; and to perseverance, godliness; and to godliness, mutual affection; and to mutual affection, love. For if you possess these qualities in increasing measure, they will keep you from being ineffective and unproductive in your knowledge of our Lord Jesus Christ. (2 Peter 1:5–8)

Peter does not tell us that doing things in increasing measure will keep us from being ineffective and unproductive. He says we must "possess these qualities." Qualities are not items on a to-do list but effects of the ongoing transformational experience.

We try to counter religion by doing more. In the relationship Jesus offers, qualities are imparted in increasing measure, and the result is effectiveness and productivity.

> But the fruit of the Spirit is love, joy, peace, forbearance, kindness, goodness, faithfulness, gentleness and self-control. Against such things there is no law. (Galatians 5:22–23)

These qualities describe who we will become. When the fruit of self-control is formed, we will exercise self-control. Instead of trying to form the fruit, we should focus on the cause that results in the fruit. When we *experience* the fruit of the Spirit, we will *express* the fruit of the Spirit.

RESURRECTION POWER

> I pray that the eyes of your heart may be enlightened in order that you may know the hope to which he has

called you, the riches of his glorious inheritance in his holy people, and his incomparably great power for us who believe. That power is the same as the mighty strength he exerted when he raised Christ from the dead and seated him at his right hand in the heavenly realms, far above all rule and authority, power and dominion, and every name that is invoked, not only in the present age but also in the one to come. (Ephesians 1:18–21)

Religion tells us that only the spirit is born again therefore our sinful nature, sinful desires, and resulting selfishness cannot be controlled by the Spirit of God. If the spirit is born again, the consequences are that we experience the power of God to overcome sin, love others, and live in unity. Relationship integrates the three dimensions in humanity.

Resurrection power is not what we feel or something we can generate intellectually but is a consequential outcome of God in us. If we are in a relationship with Christ, then we will experience His resurrection power to progressively grow in His lifestyle. Power cannot flow through us until we experience the Person empowering us from within.

The explosive power of God rebirths the human spirit, transforms the human mind, and enables the human body to know the resurrection power so we can experience true spirituality. The more we grow in cognitively experiencing God, the more we experience the metric of resurrection power.

Love Metrics

A beautiful outcome that the cross of Christ produces in humanity is love. This is a cornerstone metric for God because love reflects His nature and encompasses all His laws. Just as sin and its power were *broken* on the cross, the ability to love was *born* on the cross, enabling to be a person of love irrespective of the object of love.

All humanity is the object of God's love, which is not based on race, religion, denomination, or color. Jesus' life on earth was characterized by an unconditional love that touched every human being, no matter who they were. Love is a function of who the person becomes and not a function of the person to be loved. Religion loves people based on the quality of the person being loved. Relationship loves people based on who we become and not based on the person being loved. We do not commit actions of love to have the quality of love, for love is an outcome of transformation. Love is not what we do but who we become.

When the Spirit of God takes up residence in and transforms us to the image of Christ, we become people of love who love all people. When we experience the love of God, we are transformed into a person of love. When there is a selective expression of love, this is a religious indicator that love has not been formed in us as a metric but is being followed as a legalistic rule.

When love is seen as a rule to be followed and an act to be done this is driven by an intellectual understanding of God. When love is experienced, when we receive the love of the Father, loving others becomes an overflow of who we are. When we have the metric of love in us, we will love those around us, irrespective of the object of love. A mango cannot decide its sweetness and flavor based on the color of the skin or the religion of the person who eats the fruit! In Christ, we will progressively grow to become people of love just like Jesus, as He is the Perfection of love. The journey of Christianity is not to increase acts of love but to grow in the nature of love.

The Community of God

Dear friends, let us love one another, for love comes from God. Everyone who loves has been born of God and knows God. Whoever does not love does not know God, because God is love. This is how God showed his love among us: He sent his one and only Son into the world that we might live through him. This is love: not that we loved God, but that he loved us and sent his Son as an atoning sacrifice for our sins. Dear friends, since God so loved us, we also ought to love one another. No one has ever seen God; but if we love one another, God lives in us and his love is made complete in us. (1 John 4:7–12)

John talks about how God living in us creates a real and active love for His community. God's love is evidenced in Jesus, and God living in us is expressed by our love. We do not prove God lives in us by loving others; rather, we love others because God lives in us. The difference is what separates religion from relationship.

Religion makes loving others a methodology for proof, while relationship makes love an expressed outcome of an inner transformational experience.

Religion changes our behavior, while relationship transforms our nature.

The difference between these two is measurable, so we can know whether we are immersed in religion or saturated in a relationship. Immersion is outside in, while saturation is inside out.

The invisible God is made visible when we love one another through our experience of the Father's love. When we experience the evidence of love on the inside, we will express this by living a life of love on the outside, regardless of circumstances.

> If I speak in the tongues of men or of angels, but do not have love, I am only a resounding gong or a clanging cymbal. If I have the gift of prophecy and can fathom all mysteries and all knowledge, and if I have a faith that can move mountains, but do not have love, I am nothing. If I give all I possess to the poor and give over my body to hardship that I may boast, but do not have love, I gain nothing. Love is patient, love is kind. It does not envy, it does not boast, it is not proud. It does not dishonor others, it is not self-seeking, it is not easily angered, it keeps no record of wrongs. Love does not delight in evil but rejoices with the truth. It always protects, always trusts, always hopes, always perseveres. (1 Corinthians 13:1–7)

We can speak great spiritual truths, express spiritual gifts, display awesome faith, and give away all we have—none of this means anything in and of itself. Every religion identifies and promotes these virtues. This is what religion is all about. Talking more, having more, and giving more define twenty-first-century Christianity. We speak about what we do not understand, we have what does not fulfill, and we give what we do not have.

A relationship with God first creates an outcome inside us. We become patient and kind rather than envious, boastful, proud, and self-seeking. We become people who do not delight in evil but who always protect, trust, hope, and persevere.

> "By this everyone will know that you are my disciples, if
> you love one another." (John 13:35)

Jesus loved His disciples, so He set the metric for them to love one another. Do we define discipleship the way Jesus did? What methodologies do we use to show the world we are His disciples? Religion says we prove we are disciples by the action of love. Relationship makes us disciples so we will love unconditionally.

THE COMMUNITY OF THE WORLD

> But I tell you, love your enemies and pray for those who
> persecute you, that you may be children of your Father in
> heaven. He causes his sun to rise on the evil and the good,
> and sends rain on the righteous and the unrighteous. If you
> love those who love you, what reward will you get? Are not
> even the tax collectors doing that? And if you greet only
> your own people, what are you doing more than others? Do
> not even pagans do that? (Matthew 5:44–47)

Jesus is talking in the context of Judaism and might well be asking, "Do the Hindus and Muslims not also love their own?" He is telling the disciples that loving one's own kind is common in all religions. Even terrorist organizations around the world today demonstrate laying down their lives for a cause and beliefs. Loving those who love us is not a virtue, but loving those who are *not* like us is! Jesus is making it very clear that just loving your own is not what He is about.

Twenty-first-century Christians are quick to quote passages in James and John about not loving the world. Jesus is not teaching His disciples to love the world's *ways* but to love the world's *people*, even those who may hate them. Who does that?! James and John are referring to the worldly system that has operated since our original design was distorted.

Twenty-first-century Christians privately love the world's system and hate the world's people. We glorify the individual, the accumulation of wealth, and lavish lifestyles by selling the gospel but hate the people who oppose our faith. Authentic Christian disciples love the people who hate and persecute them. The cross of Jesus sets in place a new standard—loving all people, irrespective of who they are.

> If you really keep the royal law found in Scripture, "Love your neighbor as yourself," you are doing right. But if you show favoritism, you sin and are convicted by the law as lawbreakers. (James 2:8–9)

Loving our neighbor is the pinnacle of Christian expression. If we are unable to express love to the person we *can* see, there is no value in expressing love to the person we *cannot* see. The world knows exactly what acts of love look like, but what it needs to see are people who will regularly and consistently express love.

While actions are important, attitude and character are more important. This is what differentiated Jesus from the Pharisees, the teachers of the law who performed acts of love. Their doing was right, but their being was wrong. Jesus' actions were motivated by both the attitude and character of love. The new creation does not make us merely do-gooders but transforms us to become good. This is what we long for. Doing good may make us feel and look good on the outside, but becoming good actually makes us good on the inside. Doing good is circumstantial and situational. Being good supersedes situations, circumstances, and emotions. Doing good is selective, while becoming good is consistent.

We think love is doing what others expect us to do and agreeing to what others say. The people loved Jesus because He lived a lifestyle of communion, communication, and companionship with the Father that they all wanted but could not live. The prostitute, tax collector, Samaritan woman, leper, and sinners all saw hope in Jesus as He showed them a better way by living with them but refusing to do what they did or go along with their values. Jesus demonstrated that we can have friends in the world while living counter-culturally. This is true spiritual transformation. This is what real spiritual relationship looks like.

The Jesus lifestyle is not an agenda to fulfill, a ministry to undertake, a project to accomplish, or a mission trip to be taken. Jesus' life was not the result of an organizational plan but was an expression of who He was. Today, He calls us and promises to transform us to become like Him.

Jesus was called the "friend of sinners" (Matthew 11:19; Luke 7:34), though He remained obedient to God during His life on earth. This is real life. This is real love. This is who we will become!

THE METRIC OF UNITY

His purpose was to create in himself one new humanity out of the two, thus making peace, and in one body to reconcile both of them to God through the cross, by which he put to death their hostility. He came and preached peace to you who were far away and peace to those who were near. For through him we both have access to the Father by one Spirit. (Ephesians 2:15–18)

The greatest division that existed in biblical times was the racial divide between the Israelites and everyone else. Through the cross of Christ, God reconciled this division. Not only this, but He created a new humanity. Identities were no longer separated in terms of Jew or Gentile. In the new creation, the sole identity was now being a child of God.

There is neither Jew nor Gentile, neither slave nor free, nor is there male and female, for you are all one in Christ Jesus. If you belong to Christ, then you are Abraham's seed, and heirs according to the promise. (Galatians 3:28–29)

The context in which Paul is writing drives home the incredible unity the cross of Christ produces in the human race. This has never been more relevant than today.

Social networks are a great example of human division. I know of individuals who have multiple identities on multiple platforms on social media. Jesus created *one* network—the body of Christ. His cross created *one* human identity—the child of God.

> If someone else thinks they have reasons to put confidence in the flesh, I have more: circumcised on the eighth day, of the people of Israel, of the tribe of Benjamin, a Hebrew of Hebrews; in regard to the law, a Pharisee; as for zeal, persecuting the church; as for righteousness based on the law, faultless. But whatever were gains to me I now consider loss for the sake of Christ. What is more, I consider everything a loss because of the surpassing worth of knowing Christ Jesus my Lord, for whose sake I have lost all things. (Philippians 3:4–8)

This is a key metric of the new creation. Religion defines, defends, and divides who we are by race, denomination, culture, language, and geography. A relationship with Jesus unites humanity under one identity and enables people to celebrate the diversity of human life. The cross of Christ produces this outcome, a non-negotiable metric birthed in mankind. The unity among God's children is the same unity that Jesus, the Spirit, and the Father have. When there is disunity among those who call themselves followers of Christ, it is a symptom of the religion called Christianity.

God is raising up a generation that is fed up with self-seeking religion. They desire to experience Him beyond mere belief. When this generation begins the journey of experiencing God, the result will be a global movement that rises above the divisive religious barriers of the current times. This movement will be led *by* Christ—not be a monument built *to* Him. Members of this movement will make God their King and themselves His equal and loyal subjects. Their identity will be solely sons and daughters of the Father. Loving one another will be their foundational principle, and they will end religious divisions based on denomination, nationality, race, color, and social strata.

The evidence of Christianity is the identity of God's child, and the expression of this experience is unity in the midst of diversity. One cannot call himself or herself a Christian and divide humanity based on race, color, geography, denomination, or language. Jesus is building a united humanity that is an expression of a common identity called the children of God.

METHODOLOGY OF THE NEW CREATION

The life of Jesus on earth demonstrated how people will live as new creations. The cross—the ultimate symbol of public shame and ridicule—of Jesus, along with His suffering, death, and resurrection is the methodology of God to enable human beings to experience a relationship of communication, communion, and companionship with Him.

Christianity does not tell human beings what to do but creates the methodology for experiencing the metrics that the cross produces as a consequence of a relationship with God. Religion *demands* behavior, while relationship *enables* experiencing the metrics. Religion instructs people to do what Jesus did while relationship invites people to become like Jesus so that what Jesus did will become an overflow. The more we become like Jesus, the more we will behave like Jesus.

The methodology is not about what we do or what God does. Such a transactional approach is religion. Relationship is a response and counter-response of love. The cross of Christ triggers a response, demands a response, and this consequentially births the love of God in human beings. When the supernatural relationship starts, God takes human beings on an amazing transformational journey of love.

But how do we experience the metrics of the new creation? This methodology outlined here enables us to experience the cross as the process by which a historical event becomes a present reality. The life, suffering, death, and resurrection of Jesus are major historical events. This truth is validated when we experience the metrics of the new creation. A Christian's new present life is the evidence for Christ's historical and present life.

RE-BIRTH PROCESS

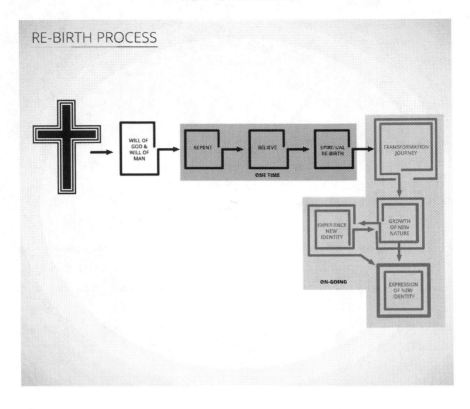

REPENTANCE

The first declaration of Jesus comes when John the Baptist calls people to repent, before Christ is introduced to the world. Understanding the context of this declaration is critical.

> In those days John the Baptist came, preaching in the wilderness of Judea and saying, "Repent, for the kingdom of heaven has come near." (Matthew 3:1–2)

"In those days," the Pharisees, Sadducees, and teachers of the law kept the tradition of the Jewish religion in the temple. The concept of God was confined to race, location, and organizations. Politically, Rome was in control. Spiritually and culturally, religious denominations and Jerusalem ruled. The religious system controlled all that the Jews could see and hear about God. Religion focused on activity as they waited for the Messiah to come and deliver them from Roman rule.

Against this backdrop of busyness and waiting, John tells them to repent. The methodology of a relationship with Christ starts not with a change of actions but with a change of mind.

Metanoia is Greek for repentance. *Meta* means change, while *noia* means mind. Therefore, a change of mind is repentance. John did not tell people to change their actions but to change their mind about God, because the Solution for the sin that orphaned humanity was on His way.

Repentance is a continuing state that begins when we change our minds about God, Jesus, and the cross. Repentance is a singular event in religion but never-ending in relationship. Repentance keeps us changing from the old to the new. An incredible journey of mind transformation starts regarding who we are, the people around us, and unity, diversity, sin, success, purpose, environment, and all of life.

> "Therefore let all Israel be assured of this: God has made this Jesus, whom you crucified, both Lord and Messiah." When the people heard this, they were cut to the heart and said to Peter and the other apostles, "Brothers, what shall we do?" Peter replied, "Repent and be baptized, every one of you, in the name of Jesus Christ for the forgiveness of your sins. And you will receive the gift of the Holy Spirit." (Acts 2:36–38)

When people respond to Peter by asking, "What should we do?" he tells them to repent—change their minds—about Jesus and the cross, the starting point for true spirituality.

Most of the time, we cloud and complicate our thinking about a person or an event based on our experiences. We might be the victims of people who called themselves Christians. Maybe Christians have caused us the most hurt. Are we willing to go beyond our personal experience with people to change our minds about Jesus and what He accomplished on the cross? This is an extremely important step in the methodology of experiencing the new creation.

In twenty-first-century Christianity, repentance has become a bad word. It's not "spiritually correct." Many today, even in the church, avoid using the word altogether. Imagine a world where we cannot change our minds about anything. Change cannot become a reality if our minds refuse to embrace it.

When we make spiritual change a constant, the variables in our minds and bodies are put into perspective. What happens to us and around us is in a state of constant change. What happens in us enables us to endure what happens to us and around us. Jesus said there is celebration in Heaven when one sinner *repents* (Luke 15:10). Interesting that He did not say when one sinner *believes*. Unless there is a change of mind about Jesus, there can be no belief in Jesus.

BELIEF

For God so loved the world that he gave his one and only Son, that whoever believes in him shall not perish but have eternal life. (John 3:16)

This statement Jesus made is likely the most quoted, yet misunderstood and misrepresented, Scripture today. Twenty-first-century Christianity has made the concept of belief into an abstract, stand-alone, futuristic pie-in-the-sky fantasy with no present consequential or transformational evidence in the mind or body. The religion of Christianity has made a statement of belief in Jesus as a stand-alone criteria for salvation.

Belief is always followed up with action. A cause triggered in a person results in an effect triggered by God. If there is no effect, there was no belief. When the blind man believed, his eyes were opened (John 9). When the woman who had been bleeding for many years believed and touched the hem of Jesus' robe, her healing came (Matthew 9).

The difference between the belief of demons and the belief of humans is what happens subsequent to belief. Demonic belief has no transformational consequence in the demons. Human belief in Jesus will trigger a series of transformational changes in the person.

The religion of Christianity says the gospel is good news because when we believe in Jesus, we will go to Heaven after death. In the relationship that Jesus came to establish, the gospel is good news because when we believe in Jesus, the eternal life of God is re-birthed in us right here on earth.

Biblical Christianity is so unique because there is a cause and effect principle at work right here, right now. Belief in Jesus is the cause that results in a series of effects. The effect is not just a one-time assurance of a futuristic event called Heaven but also a spiritual re-birth in the individual that leads to a transformational journey so the individual can cognitively experience the Person of Jesus in the present!

The good news of God is encapsulated in a short sentence that has profound meaning and implication: whoever (*pas*) believes (*pisteuo*) in him will have (*echo*) eternal (*aionios*) life (*zoe*).

Pas in Greek is an all-inclusive term with synonyms such as *every, everything, all,* and *the whole.* The cross is presented to everyone in the world, making humanity God's target group. This is not a Western political ideology, a denominational theology, or church philosophy. There is no racial or communal tone here. The cross is unique as the greatest symbol of inclusiveness, bringing everyone in the world together through the saving work of Jesus. It is such a contradiction in twenty-first-century Christianity that so many of those who take on the name of Jesus are the most divisive people!

Pisteuo, or *believes*, is similar to *faith* or *pistis*. They have the same root word in Greek—*peitho. Merriam-Webster* defines *belief* as "conviction of the truth of some statement or the reality of some being or phenomenon especially when based on examination of *evidence."* Belief without consequential transformational evidence is no belief. The reality of this God as a Being who expressed Himself through His Son Jesus transforms us through the Holy Spirit into His likeness and image. It is this evidence of transformation that validates my belief. Belief is then validated by an examination of the evidence of a transformed life.

> Now faith is the assurance (title deed, confirmation) of things hoped for (divinely guaranteed), and the evidence of things not seen [the conviction of their reality—faith comprehends as fact what cannot be experienced by the physical senses]. (Hebrews 11:1 AMP)

> Now faith is *confidence (hypostasis)* in what we hope for and *assurance (elegchos)* about what we do not see. (Hebrews 11:1, parenthetical material added)

Hypostasis is an underlying reality or substance, as opposed to that which lacks substance. *Elegchos* is a proof, that by which a thing is proved or tested. So what is faith?

Belief in Jesus Christ and His finished work on the cross results in an internal evidence that enables us, empowers us to see the unseen. There is an inner objective evidence of the unseen. The more we grow in the internal ability to see the unseen, the more we grow in faith. The more we grow in faith, the more we will be expressing faith. Evidence of the unseen in the spiritual dimension gives us confidence of the unseen in the intellectual (mind) dimension, and we then express the qualities of the unseen through the physical (body) dimension.

The writer of Hebrews puts it this way in 11:27, "By faith he [Moses] left Egypt, not fearing the king's anger; he persevered because he saw him who is invisible." The word *saw* in Greek is *horao*. One of the biblical usages is, to see with the mind or perceive. Moses had an inner perception of what he could not see with his physical eyes. This is the awareness of God in mankind partaking in the divine nature of God Himself. This is biblical Christianity. This is the disruption of life!

Jesus testified based on His internal experiential evidence of the Father. The disciples believed and were able to experience the same evidence. People who heard the disciples then believed and were also able to experience the evidence. Over the last two thousand years, belief was evidenced and declared. Therefore, people believed and the experience continued. My testimony of the experiential reality of God becomes your evidence to believe. When you believe and experience the experiential reality of God, it becomes the evidence for another to believe and experience and the cycle continues. The early church operated in this methodology. People witnessed God in the disciples, believed, and witnessed God in themselves for others to then believe and witness God.

Over the last thirty years, we have systematically disconnected belief and evidence. We have disconnected faith and its internal implications. James said in chapter 2 that "faith without works is dead" and so we went about *being* dead and *doing* works thinking that is faith. Any amount of activity that we do, without the journey of growing transformational evidence of God in us, has no spiritual or eternal consequences for humanity.

We must recognize that someone else's expression of evidence cannot become our own. Men and women of God have had incredible internal and experiential evidence that resulted in external expressions. The tragedy of twenty-first-century Christianity is that a generation looked at these external expressions and mimicked them, thinking these were the evidence for spirituality.

For example, an internal experiential evidence of God might result in the external expression of someone swaying his or her body while singing. For the person experiencing this, the swaying is just an expression. But for people watching from the outside, this can become the evidence of God. So others then start swaying their bodies as well, thinking this movement is the experience of the Spirit. They mimic the emotional expressions of others and fool themselves into thinking this is spirituality.

We have a generation today that mimics expressions, thinking that is the evidence of God. The other extreme, however, is a generation that stands stoic and upright to display an intellectual understanding and acknowledgment of God.

Without transformational internal evidence of experiencing God, belief in Christianity is dead. Mere belief or intellectual understanding does not get us to Heaven, but belief does bring Heaven down inside us now so we may experience God and express Heaven to those around us. This is practicing Jesus' words in Matthew 6:10, "Your kingdom come, your will be done, on earth as it is in heaven."

Why Believe?

Questioning the reason for believing in Jesus is like asking, "Why should my children return home?" They come home because that is where they belong. Whether we live in a shack or a mansion, my children return because that is their home. This fact centers on their relationship, not on any location. Believing solely for eternal life, prosperity, holy living, emotional highs, or miracles is religion. Coming home to the Father for any reason other than a relationship with Him is religion.

Therefore, we must stop making false promises, offering cultural bait to lure people into Christianity. The gospel is good news because it takes us to where we belong—a Spirit-to-spirit communion, communication, and companionship with the Father through the Holy Spirit because of Jesus. Every other promise or offer is a false gospel.

We should believe because of what God has done on our behalf and can do in us to return us to our original design. He promises to trigger the reset button, reclaiming our personal identity and redesigning us so we are becoming who we were meant to be. God promises a supernatural relationship that remains an internal constant amid external variables.

What Happens When We Believe?

The last three words Jesus uses in John 3:16 are *echo, aionios,* and *zoe*—"have eternal life."

Echo is translated as "have." The Greek form of *echo* means "to have, to hold, or to possess." One meaning in English is "a repeating sound." Repetition and possession are two meanings of the root word *echo* or *eche.*

Jesus' choice of words conveys the idea that when we believe in Him as the Son of God, we will possess, hold, or have something that is repetitive by nature. The real disruptor is what happens when we believe—the greatest evidence of Christianity. What does Jesus say we will possess or hold when we believe? The word *eternal* in the original Greek is *aionios. Life* in the original Greek is *zoe. Aionios* means "without beginning or end, that which has always been, or never to cease."

Jesus is saying that when we believe in the Son of God, we will possess or hold the eternal life of God. The Spirit of God rebirths the spirit of mankind and then becomes the vessel that holds the eternal life of God. We are designed to be carriers of the Divine with God inhabiting mankind. This is the beginning of seeing the unseen inside of us. Another dimension is opened within, re-birthed in us, and we start the journey of experiencing the unseen in us. This is the good news of Jesus. There is no greater miracle, no greater reason why Jesus came and went to the cross and rose again.

Religion says possession—God taking residence in us—is a belief. Relationship makes this a reality. A gospel where belief is preached as a ticket to Heaven where the human body holds the Holy Spirit with no relational experience, with the *aionios zoe* and transformational consequence on earth, is a false gospel. A salvation that is presented as a historical event with a futuristic hope where there is no transformational consequence in the present is a fake salvation.

> The life appeared; we have seen it and testify to it, and we proclaim to you the eternal life, which was with the Father and has appeared to us. (1 John 1:2)

Eternal life is a Person as well as a place. When we have the Person in the present, we get to spend time with Him in the future in that place. If we do not know the Person now, there is no place in the future. When we believe in Jesus, the eternal life of God is born in us. Understanding this reality is the start; experiencing this reality is life. Just as Jesus was conceived and then evidenced through Mary, the Holy Spirit is born in us by bringing alive the dead realm of the spirit and taking residence in us. This is the beginning of the eternal life of God inside a human being. The God who drove human beings out of the garden because of their choice returns to us as a result of our new choice. This is the most profound miracle in humanity.

Belief in Jesus triggers a series of events. Human beings are born in flesh from their parents and then are born again in the spirit. Belief triggers spiritual rebirth in mankind. The flesh (parents) gives birth to the flesh (child). The Spirit of God (the Father) rebirths the spirit of humanity and makes him or her the child of God. If physical birth is real, so is spiritual rebirth. We cannot say that physical birth is real but that spiritual rebirth is just a mystical concept or part of an ideology. Spiritual birth is not belief, but belief leads to spiritual birth.

We do not think ourselves into being children of God; we become children of God. Being born again is not some confident assumption but the experiential reality of God dwelling in us.

Our questions regarding identity come to an end when the Spirit of God dwells in us. "Who am I?" is answered with the human internal experience of "I am a child of God." The personal identity that defined mankind in the original creation is re-experienced in the new creation. This is not a confident assumption but an experiential reality. This is the evidence of the cross of Christ.

How Does This Supernatural
Transaction Take Place?

> For just as the Father raises the dead and gives them life,
> even so the Son gives life to whom he is pleased to give it. …
> Very truly I tell you, whoever hears my word and believes
> him who sent me has eternal life and will not be judged but
> has crossed over from death to life. Very truly I tell you, a
> time is coming and has now come when the dead will hear
> the voice of the Son of God and those who hear will live.
> For as the Father has life in himself, so he has granted the
> Son also to have life in himself. (John 5:21, 24–26)

Just as God breathed life into Adam and he became a living being, the
Son gives the life of God for the spirit of mankind to be reborn. Mankind
who has been seeking true identity finds it when the Spirit of God takes
residence within.

> Just as Moses lifted up the snake in the wilderness, so the
> Son of Man must be lifted up, that everyone who believes
> may have eternal life in him. (John 3:14–15)

When the angel told Mary that a child would be born to her, she asked
how this could be since she was still a virgin. The angel replied that the
Holy Spirit would come upon her and the power of the Most High would
overshadow her (Luke 1). When Jesus told Nicodemus he had to be born
again, Nicodemus asked the same question: "How can this be?" (John 3).

The answer was the same in both cases. The solution was from God,
who would birth life into Mary's womb. He would also birth the eternal
life of God in the human spirit. Jesus would be born in the womb, and
the Holy Spirit would rebirth the human spirit. This is the beginning of
a journey with Jesus as the Way (John 14:6). Therefore, being born again
is not a destination but the start of God's transformation of the human
mind into the mind of Christ so people can experience God. Repentance
leads to belief, belief leads to rebirth, and rebirth leads to a lifelong journey

of transformation of the mind so the reality in the spiritual dimension becomes a reality in the mind and body. A change of mind about God leads to choosing to believe in God, resulting in spiritual rebirth, leading to a transformational journey of experiencing spiritual reality in the mind.

THE GAP OF LIFE

The gap of life is the space in time from conception to manifestation.

When the sperm and egg join together in a woman's womb, when two cells unite to form a single embryo, the miracle of life occurs. For the first thirty days, even the mother does not know life has been conceived. The outside world notices the pregnancy after about four months. But from the day of conception, a two-celled embryo multiplies and grows, eventually becoming a person. This is the gap of life—the time between conception (which is invisible) to manifestation (the time where life is visible). The invisibility of life does not mean there is an absence of life.

How does this life transformation take place? Does a mother will herself into growing a child within? A mother eats, goes about her normal routine, sleeps, and chooses to take care of herself. The effect is a child growing and being transformed into who he or she is meant to be. Work on the cause, and the effect will take care of itself.

The gap of life is the time from when the seed is sown to the time we see the root and the shoot come out. We have multiple examples in everyday life, but when it comes to spirituality, we switch to our world of instant results. Since we want everything now, we then choose an artificial means to birth and experience spirituality. Not so in being born of the Spirit.

The religion called Christianity pushes people to repent, believe, and behave. Biblical Christianity invites humanity to experience God first, and this happens through the transformation of the mind. Without cognitive communication, communion, and companionship with God, all that we say and do is religion. Transformation of the mind is the process by which the reality of communication, communion, and companionship with God in the realm of the spirit is experienced by the human mind. The more we experience the Person of God, the more we express the Person of God. The more our mind becomes the mind of Christ the more Christ lives through us.

TRANSFORMATION OF THE MIND: WHAT IS TRANSFORMATION?

Metamorphosis, the biological process through which a caterpillar is transformed into a butterfly, has long been used as an analogy for the process of experiencing the new creation. Metamorphosis in biblical Christianity is transformation into the image of Jesus. This leads to the visible creation of His image in us. Transformation enables the reality of the re-birth of the spirit and co-habitation of the Holy Spirit to become an experiential reality in the mind and a consequential expression through the body, enabling us to live the Jesus lifestyle. No transformation means no Jesus, and no Jesus means no transformation.

Adam and Eve originally reflected the image of God, and through the cross we start the relational journey to recapture our spirituality so we can reflect the image of God. We become like Jesus! He is our Benchmark, Plumb Line, Metric, and Standard.

Transformation into Jesus' likeness is very different from simply imitating His actions. We are called to imitate *how* Jesus lived and not to imitate *what* Jesus did. Religion calls us to conform to *do* what Jesus did. Relationship transforms us so we become like Him. When we become like Him, we behave like Him.

Transformation of the mind is the process by which the gap of life is bridged, and we experience the internal evidences of communion, communication, and companionship of God. When we repent and believe in Jesus, there are consequential realities that happen in the realm of the spirit. These will be translocated from the spirit to the mind so the mind can experience the realities of what has happened in the spirit. This translocation from our spirit to our mind is achieved through the process called transformation of the mind. As much as the mind can recognize the body, the mind is transformed to recognize the spirit.

Returning to our previous examples of how nature demonstrates transformation, the Spirit of God rebirthing our spirit and dwelling in us is like a seed germinating. The soil is plowed and the seed sown. The seed coat absorbs the water and loosens up. Then it breaks apart and the embryo starts to grow. The radicle, which eventually becomes the root, grows first, meaning the first outward growth of a seed occurs downward. The radicle absorbs water, and the plumule, which becomes the shoot, breaks through the soil and grows upward. The invisible (the part in the soil) grows first, pushing the visible out through the soil. The root facilitates the transfer of water and nutrients from the soil. This enables transformation of the seed into a plant with the consequence of fruit. What is visible (on top of the soil) is only as good as the invisible (in the soil). It does not matter how beautiful the visible looks. If the invisible dies, the visible will eventually die.

Nature teaches us that the lasting beauty of the external depends totally on the internal. The seed coat breaking open is the rebirth of the spirit. The radicle in us is the mind. Unless the mind recognizes and understands the Spirit, there is no growth. As much as the radicle, or the root, needs to pierce into the soil for nourishment, the mind and the Spirit of God need to be interconnected. This is where the problem in the religion of Christianity begins. We repent, believe, and then try to act like who we are supposed to become. The mind tries to follow the rules of the Spirit without first being transformed by the Spirit. Jesus did not come to give us a new set of rules to follow. He came so the Spirit of God, which is the life of God, can transform us to the image of God again.

In our plant example, what if the shoot looks up at the world, sees the other trees and fruits, and imitates those trees and fruits? The shoot will try to grow faster than the root. What the shoot wants and what the root wants now conflict. Instead of growing downward to establish strong roots, the radicle will try to grow upward to create fruit.

But if the radicle pushes downward, absorbing water and nutrients to transport upward, the shoot will push up and be transformed into an amazing plant. When there is life in the seed, the radicle and plumule must germinate and grow. If there is life in the seed, the journey of transformation from seed to fruit will happen as a consequence. If there is rebirth of the spirit of mankind, then transformation of the mind is a consequence. The evidence of spiritual rebirth is the journey of transformation of the mind.

> Therefore, there is now no condemnation for those who are in Christ Jesus, because through Christ Jesus the law of the Spirit who gives life has set you free from the law of sin and death. (Romans 8:1–2)

CAUSE AND EFFECT PRINCIPLE

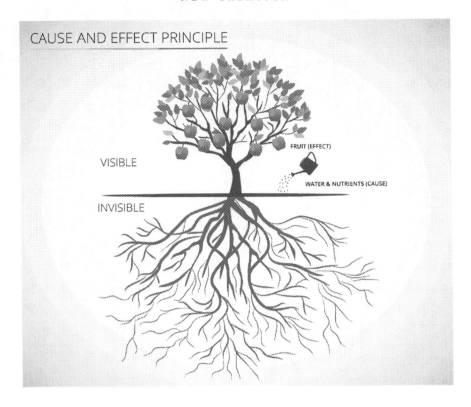

When the human spirit is born again, a new operating principle comes into play. From the state of sin and death that ruled us, we are co-inhabited by the Spirit of God. The new birth by the cross is not only another dimension in us but also a wholly new methodology for living on earth. After living through our minds and bodies, we can now live from a new dimension of the Spirit. We have a source change with a new power and new life. We now hold what we did not have through belief, but we won't automatically experience the implications of what happens in us when we believe. Because we have lived so long in the old methodology of our mind being the source, the experience of the new will come only by transformation of the mind, which will enable us to live from the new Source. This is what Christianity is all about, moving out of living from our minds and bodies to live from the Spirit.

Who I am is defined in the dimension of the spirit and cognitively experienced in the mind and body through transformation. The dimension of the spirit defines sonship identity, the mind cognitively experiences this identity of adoption, and the body of the individual expresses this inner experience. This is one of the most incredible experiences that humanity longs for. This becomes a reality through transformation of the mind as the bridge that interconnects the dimension of God and our dimensions.

Transformation changes theology into biography and theory into experience.

+ Belief leads to rebirth.
+ Rebirth leads to new life.
+ New life leads to the Spirit influencing the mind.
+ The Spirit's influence on the mind leads to transformation.
+ Transformation of the mind leads to God's image being formed in us.
+ God's image enables us to experience our new identity as children of God.
+ Experiencing God results in expressing God's nature to the world around us.

The cross of Christ triggers all these truths as a series of consequences. We cannot simply stay at belief but will move to transformation, which enables us to experience what we believe. This transformation is fundamental in biblical Christianity, enabling us to experience what Christ achieved on the cross. If there is no transformation, then it means there is no belief. This is a directly co-relating cause-and-effect principle.

Christianity is not an illogical belief system but a cognitively real inter-dimensional experiential relationship that we all long for. Transformation of the mind is the methodology of humanity being enabled to partake in the divine nature of God without the entrapments of religion. There is no Hollywood-style special effects, nor is there an emotional frenzy that has come to define some aspects of Christianity today. Transformation of the mind means humanity gets back to who we were always meant to be.

THE RATE OF TRANSFORMATION: THE JOURNEY OF DISCIPLESHIP

And we all, who with unveiled faces contemplate the Lord's glory, are being transformed into his image with

> ever-increasing glory, which comes from the Lord, who is
> the Spirit. (2 Corinthians 3:18)

Joseph was forgotten in prison for more than ten years. Moses lived a solitary and isolated life for forty years. After being anointed as king, David did not sit on the throne for thirty years. Paul was sent away to be on his own for a season after his conversion.

Religion demands immediate performance of perfection, while relationship enables transformation over time through real-life circumstances. There are some plants that go from germination to fruiting in thirty days, while some take two years. What matters is whether there is growth and continuous translocation of water and nutrients from the soil into the plant.

Twenty-first-century Christianity does not allow people to be vulnerable during this transformational growth process, because we define our faith by what we do and do not do by whether we become like Christ. I know people who instantly experience the cognitive reality of God when they repent and believe with instant expression of their inner reality. I also know people who have taken years for this to occur. What is important is to be on the journey of transformation.

The church is a sanctuary where we can reveal who we are beneath the mask of the flesh, knowing we will be accepted and encouraged towards transformation. The early church was a beautiful community of imperfect people being perfected by the perfect Person, journeying together toward greater maturity. There is a beautiful balance the cross births in the church. On one side, it does not condemn, and on the other, it does not condone. We need to neither act perfect nor resign to a lifestyle of imperfection. All the letters in the New Testament written to churches have one objective: to encourage individuals to become like Jesus. Today, the church has become a place for perfect hypocrites rather than imperfect people to be transformed from their hypocrisy to experiencing their true identity in the spirit.

Every Christian home can become this safe place where parents display their vulnerability and avoid creating an artificially perfect state so their children do not become Christian actors inside the home while living like the devil in the outside world. We can create a community that rejects a false status of sinless perfection, which is in itself sin, and knows the metrics, encouraging and building up members through transformational methodologies and keeping them accountable through measurements. This safe and secure place does not exist in religion but thrives in relationship!

Discipleship is conventionally understood as intentional steps toward spiritual growth to live a mature Christian lifestyle. For decades, discipleship programs have laid out behavioral standards and attempted to force people to meet them. The Greek word for discipleship is *mathetes*, meaning pupil or learner. This is an ancient Eastern concept. The pupil spends time with the teacher, learning from the teacher, and then becomes like the teacher. The cause is the teacher and the disciple being together. The effect is the disciple becoming like the teacher and, therefore consequentially, behaving like the teacher. There is a relationship established where the teacher and the pupil start doing life together.

Being together takes precedence over *doing*. When the being together happens, there is a transformational learning in the disciple. The disciple begins to think like the teacher. Transformational thinking leads to a transformational lifestyle in line with the teacher. The methodology of transformation is Christian discipleship. This is not a weekend event, but a lifelong journey.

Jesus called His followers to be disciples, not simply believers. A person could meet Jesus and believe in Him only to go on selfishly about life now knowing He exists. But the disciples lived with Jesus and were focused on Him. Belief is certainly the first step toward discipleship, but belief by itself does not make someone a disciple. Believers do not go to Heaven, disciples do!

> And I will ask the Father, and he will give you another advocate to help you and be with you forever—the Spirit of truth. The world cannot accept him, because it neither sees him nor knows him. But you know him, for he lives with you and will be in you. (John 14:16–17)

Jesus is talking to His disciples just before going to the cross, knowing He will soon be with them only in the spiritual realm.

After His resurrection, Jesus commands His disciples to wait. A stunning change lies ahead. He will return and take up residence in them through the Holy Spirit. He would go from living *with* His disciples to living *in* them! It is important to note that the disciples did not go about trying to replicate the "rushing wind" and "tongues of fire" expressions in the early church. Their focus was to bring people to experience God living in them. This is the incredible truth of the cross. The experiential reality of God in mankind happens in discipleship—the transformation of the mind so He can live in relationship with human beings. Humanity actually gets to be with and connect to God here on earth.

Discipleship is a journey, and journeys happen over time. May we move from the world of instant members to the incredible journey of discipleship, which is what Christianity is all about.

SPIRITUAL OXYGEN—THE RAW MATERIAL FOR TRANSFORMATION

Today, for a vast majority of the global population, the Christian Scriptures are a history book. For a greater majority of the Christian population, the Bible goes one step further and is a set of instructions from God for humanity. Depending on the audience, it has also become a motivational tool, bedtime story, and legal reference guide. Indeed, the Bible has many uses inside and outside Christianity.

The Pharisees knew the Word of God. Satan has it memorized, even quoting it to Jesus. Therefore, using or reading the Scriptures does not make one spiritual. Religious systems use the Bible to teach principles that lead to a good and godly life while having no spiritual impact. While the Scriptures are not God, their impact in our lives is directly related to how we view its pages. A correct understanding of the Bible is critical if it is to have an experiential effect. Like repentance, a change of mind about the Christian Scriptures is of greater importance than a change of lifestyle.

Twenty-first-century Christians often read the Bible simply to support certain actions, denominational theories, and ideologies. Allowing the Word to transform us is different from using the Word to justify our ideas, even if it is about faith and salvation. The former is relationship; the latter is religion. What the Word does in us is of greater importance than how much theoretical knowledge of God we have. Reading the Word is important, but if it is a checklist that we mark every day, there is no transformational influence.

We live in a time where there is great revelation leading to eloquent exposition of the Bible. Never before in the history of humanity have we seen such large amounts of incredible content created around the themes of the Scriptures. But revelation that is not translated into personal experience has no spiritual value. The Pharisees of Jesus' time had great knowledge, but they were men with human minds understanding spiritual matters and they were not allowing God's Spirit to reveal truth to them leading to transformation.

In Matthew 6, Jesus said, "Do not worry." We go about memorizing this verse, declaring and quoting the words to ourselves like a chant, desperately trying not to worry. The mind takes the Word and tries to reinforce the truth of Scripture back into the mind. Jesus ends that teaching by saying the Father knows your needs and He will give us what we need. This is an inter-dimensional relationship and not a transaction of the mind. Between the statements of knowing and giving, Jesus tells His audience to seek His Kingdom and His righteousness. Seeking His Kingdom is seeking His influence in our lives, like Adam in the original design. Seeking His righteousness is letting the righteousness of God be unraveled in our lives, as Adam prior to the fall was righteous before God and in himself.

These are inter-dimensional and relational journeys that Jesus is asking His followers to seek and experience. Where there is no inter-dimensional transfer of knowledge, it is religion. Jesus said it this way in Matthew 16:17: "Blessed are you, Simon son of Jonah, for this was not revealed to you by flesh and blood, but by my Father in heaven." Revelation by the Spirit has internal transformational consequences, while theoretical understanding of the mind has external behavioral consequences just like the Pharisees.

The Bible becomes inspiration depending on our intent and attitude. When Jesus was on earth, He had two kinds of audiences outside his disciples—the people of the world and the people of the religious system. Both heard the same Word. The first audience experienced its effect, with the supernatural breaking through into the natural, but the second audience was unmoved. The difference was the motive and intent of the mind. The same Word spoken in the same context had a different impact based on the approach the listener took. The Pharisees listened to the same Word as those who were healed. Some got furious, while others were freed.

The Pharisees and Sadducees saw Jesus through their denominational filters. One believed in resurrection, and the other did not. The teachings of Jesus did not make sense to them because what they heard and what they had been taught to believe about God contradicted. There can be no human leader, irrespective of their greatness, who can influence anyone on biblical paradigms other than the Word of God itself. Intentionally removing our cultural, racial, denominational, and traditional biases is foundational for the Word to have transformational impact in our lives. Like microwaving a precooked meal, we want someone else to digest the Bible for us. But spirituality does not work that way. There can be no intermediaries at any level in this relationship that Jesus came to establish.

> The Spirit gives life; the flesh counts for nothing. The words I have spoken to you—they are full of the Spirit and life. (John 6:63)

We have seen that belief results in *echo aionios zoe*, having eternal life. In the above verse, Jesus contrasts the role of the flesh and the role of the Spirit, or *pneuma. Pneuma zoopoieo* in Greek is the Spirit forming, creating, or producing *zoo, zao,* or *zoe,* meaning life. He goes on to say that the word *rhema* He has spoken is Spirit and life. The Word of God does not *contain* life but *is* life. His Word has the capacity to create life in human beings. The Bible is the oxygen the Spirit of God uses for rebirth and transformation. The Holy Spirit uses the Word of God to transform the human mind into the mind of Christ. All cognitive experience of the Spirit is made possible by and through the Word of God. The Word is the cause, transformation is the effect, and conformance to be like Jesus is the experience.

> "We have come to believe and to know that you are the Holy One of God." (John 6:69)

The word *know* is translated from two Greek words, *oida* and *ginosko. Oida* means "knowing about." *Ginosko* means "experiential knowledge." While demons *oida* (know) about Jesus, His children *ginosko* (have a real connection to Him). *Ginosko* is a Jewish idiom for intimacy between man and woman. The religion of Christianity is to *"oida"* God. Relationship in Christianity is to *"ginosko"* God. The Word of God moves us from *oida* (knowing about) to *ginosko* (relationally intimate).

BIBLICAL SEQUENCE

There is a new grid by which the Christian Scriptures are to be read and understood. The Bible consists of sixty-six books—thirty-nine before the coming of Jesus, or BC, and twenty-seven after the coming of Jesus, or AD.

> These things happened to them as examples for us. They were written down to warn us who live at the end of the age. (1 Corinthians 10:11 NLT)

The Scriptures written prior to Jesus' birth teach about God's pursuit of humanity for a relationship of love so He may act in us as well as on our behalf. There is an inter-dimensional teaching throughout the Christian Scriptures. In the first thirty-nine books, the spiritual dimension of God engages with the dimension of mind and body in humanity. The Spirit of God comes into the natural dimension of mankind. For example, where God engages with Moses in the burning bush. The Spirit of God also comes into the spiritual dimension in humans, like the prophets. God constantly made inter-dimensional contact with humanity.

The Scriptures written after Jesus teach about the reality of the supernatural dimension, about Him, why He came, what He achieved, and how humanity may again partake in the divine nature. The New Testament Scriptures teach us the reality of experiencing God in humanity where the Spirit of God takes up residence and does not come and go. The supreme teaching of the Bible is the desire of God to have a relationship of love with humanity and restore us to the original design while here on earth where God and man live in communion, communication, and companionship.

Subsequent to the resurrection of Jesus, the Spirit of God gains residence in humanity when there is repentance and belief. There is no coming in and going out, but the objective of the New Testament teaching is to enable humanity to experience the Spirit of God taking residence in humanity. The Word of God first teaches the reality of what happens in the spiritual realm of humanity and then, second, how that manifests itself in and through us. Grasping this sequence is incredibly important. Unless we understand the reality of God in the *invisible* realm then what the cross has achieved on our behalf in the invisible is impossible to experience and express in the reality of God in the *visible*. Inspiration leads to transformation and then follows instruction.

The Scriptures written after Jesus also generally follow a particular pattern. For example, Romans chapters 1 to 7 teach the reality of sin, the power of the cross, and its implication in humanity. Chapter 8 teaches the methodology of how the historical reality of the cross becomes a present experience. Chapters 10 to 16 teach how internal evidence expresses itself externally. This is a consistent process that all writers of the epistles follow: inspiration, transformation, and then consequential instruction on expression.

There is a new paradigm through which the Bible needs to be studied: not as an instruction manual but to learn how the spiritual dimension interplays with the mind and body. The Pharisees started with what we should do (instruction), but Jesus starts with who we should become (inspiration and transformation).

The Role of the Word of God in Mankind

> All Scripture is God-breathed and is useful for teaching, rebuking, correcting and training in righteousness, so that the servant of God may be thoroughly equipped for every good work. (2 Timothy 3:16–17)

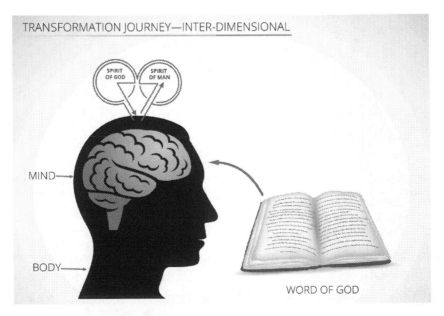

Good works—the moral and social compass of Jesus in us—result from being thoroughly equipped and trained in righteousness through the Word of God. We do not do the right things *to become* righteous. We do the right things because *we become* righteous. The renewal of the mind through the Word of God helps us to think right so we can behave right.

The Word of God accomplishes this in us by renewing the mind, making the transition from our old to new nature possible. Without this training and equipping, we will keep trying to do good works in our own strength. The Word of God is the methodology of the cross of Christ to transform our mind to the mind of Christ so we may experience God beyond mere belief, become transformed to become like Him, and therefore consequentially live like Him.

> Do not merely listen to the word, and so deceive yourselves. Do what it says. Anyone who listens to the word but does not do what it says is like someone who looks at his face in a mirror and, after looking at himself, goes away and immediately forgets what he looks like. But whoever looks intently into the perfect law that gives freedom, and continues in it—not forgetting what they have heard, but doing it—they will be blessed in what they do. (James 1:22–25)

When we act from a position of who we are not, it is like looking in a mirror and when we walk away, we forget who we are. James is not telling us simply to act out what the Word says. The Greek word used for the phrase *look intently* is *parakypto*. This is "a posture, an act, event, or occasion," meaning to "stoop to look with head bowed forward." The phrase *continues in it* in the Greek is *parameno*. *Meno* is the word Jesus used when He said, "Abide in me." The Greek word for the phrase *doing it* is *poietes*, which means a "maker, producer, or an author."

James is saying that when we read the Word of God and let it abide in us, we will be transformed to become producers. We will be blessed because we will produce from whom we become. Doing is a consequence of looking intently into the Word of God. When we consistently read the Word, the Spirit uses it to renew our minds so we produce what God wants us to produce. We do not act like producers; we become producers from an action of the Spirit, because of the Word of God. There is no imitation here, only an absolutely new creation formed from within.

> Jesus answered, "It is written: 'Man shall not live on bread alone, but on every word that comes from the mouth of God.'" (Matthew 4:4)

As the Word became flesh, Jesus used the written Word of God and quoted from Deuteronomy to stop the Enemy. What bread does in the physical realm, the Word does for our spirits and our minds. Physical bread transforms us from two-celled beings to multi-celled men or women. The "bread of the Spirit" is the Word of God, which transforms us so we may experience communication, communion, and companionship of the Father.

The Principle of Beholding

> And we all, who with unveiled faces contemplate the Lord's glory, are being transformed into his image with ever-increasing glory, which comes from the Lord, who is the Spirit. (2 Corinthians 3:18)

"We all" are those who have taken the first two steps—repentance and belief. This is like the seed coat of a new plant breaking open, the sperm and the egg coming together, or a wedding day.

Rebirth of the spirit puts humanity in a position to engage with the dimension of God. The word *contemplate* in Greek is *katoptrizo*, meaning to "behold as in a mirror." In my work with prisoners and their children, our objective is to ensure the kids do not follow the parent's self-destructive path. The methodology we use is to build a right relationship between the inmate and his child. Sadly, in far too many cases, a child brought to a father does not recognize him. The father looks into the child's face, but the child looks confused. These are always awkward moments. But over time, the child warms up to the father, bonding occurs, love breaks forth, and often, by the end of the day, the child doesn't want to leave him.

The same process occurs with us. There is a progressive experiential recognition of God in our minds. This is *mathetes*, or discipleship—the Father and child spending time together. There is an inner temple within a human being where God and mankind commune, communicate, and have companionship. The Spirit of God embraces the mind of the individual, and there is an intimacy of love experienced. No human vocabulary can articulate this brand of love. As the Spirit of God takes the Word of God and transforms the mind of a person to the mind of Christ, this cognitive experience of God then grows.

> I keep asking that the God of our Lord Jesus Christ, the glorious Father, may give you the Spirit of wisdom and revelation, so that you may know him better. I pray that the eyes of your heart may be enlightened in order that you may know the hope to which he has called you, the riches of his glorious inheritance in his holy people. (Ephesians 1:17–18)

In the new creation, the eyes of the heart become the inward eye, allowing us to see, understand, and become aware of the spirit realm. Just as the physical eye is the window to the physical world, the mind becomes the window or eye to the spirit. We perceive and become conscious of God in the spirit through the "eyes" of our minds.

As we continually read and retain the Word, the Spirit of God transforms our minds to *see God as He sees us*. As we continually read and retain the Word, the Spirit of God transforms our minds to see the world as God sees the world. As men like Abraham and Moses did, we can begin to see the unseen.

Temptation: Theory Becomes Experience

Teams can practice all year long, but the value of their hard work is not proven there. During the season, the games are the actual tests of the efficiency of the practice and of the players' abilities.

In the same way, knowing all about spirituality is incredibly great, but experiencing true spirituality happens on a day-to-day basis through the everyday realities of life.

> Indeed, when Gentiles, who do not have the law, do by nature things required by the law, they are a law for themselves, even though they do not have the law. They show that the requirements of the law are written on their hearts, their consciences also bearing witness, and their thoughts sometimes accusing them and at other times even defending them. (Romans 2:14-15)

Temptation is a universal constant. All of us, irrespective of our belief or unbelief in God, fight with things that we do that we do not want to do. We know the consequence of guilt, even if we try to change the laws of right and wrong. Our conscience is the natural reflector of the supernatural God. We do not need spirituality to "feel guilty." Our conscience is the programmed moral code. One suffering that exists in all of humanity from the First World to the Third World and all the cultures in between is the internal pain we experience when we grapple with the desires that we do not want to fulfill.

From when I wanted to go against my mom's instructions to take three cookies instead of two to picking up the cigarette that my dad threw away, human nature is wired to be lured into what we do not want to do. My desire was to listen to the right instructions of my dad and mom, but there was this nature in me that wanted the opposite. Whether we believe in God or not, we all experience the lure of what we know is not right but go ahead and do it anyway. That lure that leaves us with a guilty conscience is temptation. This is not solely a Christian or religious concept because humanity experiences this. Regret, guilt, remorse, and all the associated pain and destruction that is connected to our actions—when we do what we do not want to do *and* when we do what we know we should not do—is a consequence of temptation.

All of humanity handles temptation in various ways. The law of the land is a fundamental guide to how we handle temptation. Do not sell cigarettes to those who are under 18. Do not sell alcohol to those who are under 21. Cocaine possession will result in an arrest and a likely jail term. These are examples of ways the government enacts attempted management of this innate nature in humanity. But we all know that laws have not succeeded in keeping people away from the things that we do that we do not want to do and things that we do that leave a lasting effect.

The religious also have their own ways of handling temptation. A common theme in almost all religions is punishment in eternal hellfire for individuals who succumb to temptation and go against their religious beliefs. But fear of hellfire has never succeeded in helping humanity. Some religions give license to the things that we do not want to do but desire to do. Polygamy in Islam is one example. There are multiple cults and religious sects that essentially legalize temptation. Self-control, thought control, and physical discipline are various self-help methodologies that we use to manage natural desires that build up in us with the end result spanning from guilt to depression.

Humanity ultimately bears responsibility for the after-effects of drug overdoses, alcohol abuse, sexual deviances, and sinful practices that goes against our natural conscience. Just because a country legalizes cheating does not remove the inner guilt that comes from cheating. Trying to manage a legalized hangover of the conscience is both depressing and oppressive.

How we handle temptation in the new creation is a fundamental differentiator in the relationship that Jesus came to re-establish.

> How much more, then, will the blood of Christ, who through the eternal Spirit offered himself unblemished to God, cleanse our consciences from acts that lead to death, so that we may serve the living God! (Hebrews 9:14)

The cross of Jesus Christ overcomes the root problem of the sinful nature and the effects of temptation in the new creation. In the fallen creation, we go through this cycle of regret, remorse, and condemnation. In the new creation, a new methodology is formed to handle this natural lure called temptation. An inner compass called the conscience is in all of humanity. Irrespective of what positions we hold in life, this inner compass is constantly seeking for true north.

Physical pain is bad, but a conscience in pain can be unbearable. The cross of Christ sets true north inside of us and brings real rest within, one that is not contingent on external variables. Even when shackled in a prison cell, there is an inner rest that bursts out in joy; an inner rest that enables one to call out a message of peace and forgiveness when being stoned to death, as Stephen did; an inner rest that empowers us to forgive those who have hurt us. This cannot be manufactured on a Sunday morning because it is not an emotion or a knowledge but an incredible act of the Spirit of God in the conscience of the individual. The cleansing of the conscience is not a belief but an experience as a consequence of belief.

Temptations are the enemy's lure to keep our consciences in a state of guilt and inner restlessness. Temptation is anything in the realm of the mind and body that lures us to move away from the internal wholeness that God designed us to experience. The cross of Christ is the only methodology by which we are enabled to live an overcoming life with the Spirit of God cleansing our past, empowering the present to lead us into a future where there will be no need to struggle any longer with our internal conflicts.

> For in my inner being I delight in God's law; but I see another law at work in me, waging war against the law of my mind and making me a prisoner of the law of sin at work within me. (Romans 7:22-23)

An individual who is re-born in the spirit will be able to identify the three dimensions of body, mind, and spirit, gaining an understanding of the internal conflict of the new creation enabling the individual to overcome.

1. The spirit, a new inner being reborn in us, is the spiritual dimension of which the mind progressively becomes aware.
2. The mind of the individual experiences a war that is waged by the sinful nature in us.
3. The body is the aspect that keeps succumbing to the war within so the mind is the fulcrum that recognizes the spirit and also the sinful nature that war against the desires of the spirit.

In the fallen creation, the conflict exists between sin, the mind, and body. There is no awareness of the spirit or spiritual nature. The mind tries to desperately deal with the triggers of sin and the body succumbs to them, leading to guilt and depression.

In the new creation, temptation takes on a completely new dimension. This is not just a bad conscience reacting to the moral laws encoded in us but a conflict of two natures. When an individual is born again, a new creation is formed through the rebirth of the spirit, and a new nature is formed that conflicts with the old nature.

Continuing in Romans 7:24, for most people, the exasperation Paul expressed is the very lifestyle of living the religious Christian life: "What a wretched man I am! Who will rescue me from this body that is subject to death?" Many Christians tend to either give in to the law of sin or get out of the faith because the old nature seems to keep overpowering them. When we try to overcome the lure of the old nature only through the mind, Christianity becomes a burden to follow and a failed religion. And that is what religions are all about: They fail us.

Jesus came to have a relationship with us, indwell in us, and transform our minds so we might be enabled and empowered to know Him and have communion, communication, and companionship with God Himself. The unique differentiator of the cross of Christ is its ability to transform the mind so it is enabled and empowered to overcome the triggers of the old nature and live in harmony with the new nature that is birthed in and through the Spirit. He came so that unlike Adam and Eve, we will not be lured and destroyed by the enemy. The event of spiritual re-birth and the journey of transformation are tightly interconnected to learning to overcome temptation. The religion called Christianity conveniently separates re-birth from overcoming.

> But thanks be to God! He gives us the victory through our
> Lord Jesus Christ. (1 Corinthians 15:57)

A relationship with Jesus leads to the dimension of the Spirit transforming the mind so that the mind is enabled and empowered by the Spirit to live an overcoming life. We do not and cannot deliver ourselves from the old nature into the new nature. God Himself through Christ delivers us.

> Therefore, there is now no condemnation for those who
> are in Christ Jesus, because through Christ Jesus the law
> of the Spirit who gives life has set you free from the law of
> sin and death. (Romans 8:1-2)

This is the incredibly good news of the gospel of Jesus Christ. There is a new law—the law of the Spirit—that sets the re-born individual on a journey of experiencing freedom from the old law of sin and death. This is not about mind control or thought control but the Spirit-controlled mind!

> And so he condemned sin in the flesh, in order that the
> righteous requirement of the law might be fully met in us,
> who do not live according to the flesh but according to the
> Spirit. (Romans 8:3-4)

The righteous requirements of God are fully met in those who do not live according to their mind and body, but let their mind be in line with what the Spirit desires. The privilege of the righteousness of Christ being experienced in the individual is not based on an historical event called belief, but is based on a daily transformational experience of living according to the Spirit.

Threefold Transformation in Humanity: Spirit

> You, however, are not in the realm of the flesh but are in
> the realm of the Spirit, if indeed the Spirit of God lives in
> you. And if anyone does not have the Spirit of Christ, they
> do not belong to Christ. (Romans 8:9)

Paul, as a statement of fact, is telling the church in Rome that they are not just in the physical dimension, but they also are in the spiritual dimension. Their spiritual dimension has been transformed. This is not just a belief but also a reality. This is the game changer of the relationship that Jesus came to birth: the Spirit of God lives in us and we become spiritual beings.

And Paul goes on to say that those who do not have the Spirit do not belong to Christ. The religion of Christianity says if you believe in Christ then you belong to Christ. The Bible says that those who belong to Christ are those in whom the Spirit of God *lives*. Is it possible to let someone live in our home without us knowing that person actually lives? Twenty-first-century Christianity does exactly that: believe the Spirit of God lives in you, but it doesn't matter if He who lives within you interacts with you or not.

> For those who are led by the Spirit of God are the children of God. (Romans 8:14)

Those in whom the Spirit of Christ dwells and leads are the children of God. When we believe, the Spirit of God takes residence, and through this incredible relationship called the transformation of the mind, we cognitively know that He dwells in us, and we let the Spirit control our minds so the Spirit can lead us. This is the methodology for living the supernatural life, naturally!

THREEFOLD TRANSFORMATION IN HUMANITY: MIND

> Those who live according to the flesh have their minds set on what the flesh desires; but those who live in accordance with the Spirit have their minds set on what the Spirit desires. The mind governed by the flesh is death, but the mind governed by the Spirit is life and peace. (Romans 8:5-6)

There is an incredible supernatural interplay that happens in the biblical methodology of overcoming temptation. The Spirit of God takes the Word of God and transforms our minds to choose the direction of the Spirit in us and not submit to the sinful triggers within. The journey of Christianity is for us to live lives that are empowered by the Spirit to choose to stay in alignment with what God says in our spirits instead of what the enemy whispers in our ears. Our mind can choose to say 'yes' to the Spirit and 'no' to the independent triggers of the mind and body. A transformed mind is an overcoming mind. Transformation of the mind is the cause, while overcoming the selfish desires is the effect.

This is why some Bible versions use the word "aliens" to refer to those who follow God on earth. People live only from the mind and body, but a reborn human being becomes a spiritual being with a mind and body. The mind that has been programmed to respond to the triggers of the old nature and the world around begins to start operating from the Spirit. Since our physical birth, the mind lives off the nature that we have at birth. When our spirit is reborn, there is a source transformation that occurs from which the mind needs to live.

The incredible journey of Christianity is to progressively be transformed from operating from the mind to operating from the Spirit. We die to the control of the mind to live by the control of the Spirit.

THREEFOLD TRANSFORMATION IN HUMANITY: BODY

> But if Christ is in you, then even though your body is subject to death because of sin, the Spirit gives life because of righteousness. (Romans 8:10)

Jesus' suffering, death, and resurrection credit righteousness to those who follow Him. This is no fantasy. When we believe, this righteousness causes the Spirit of God to empower the body. This is a practical reality of experience and not a theoretical belief.

The religion of Christianity makes the righteousness provided by Christ on the cross something to believe. The relationship that Jesus came to birth results in the practical implications of the righteousness of Christ by empowering and enabling our bodies to overcome the destructive desires of the old nature. Sin that separated God and humanity is replaced with the righteousness of Christ. That opens the way for the Spirit of God to indwell, influence, enable, and empower the body of the individual. This is the disruption of the cross. What is insignificant in us becomes significant and displaces the old with the new.

> And if the Spirit of him who raised Jesus from the dead is living in you, he who raised Christ from the dead will also give life to your mortal bodies because of his Spirit who lives in you. (Romans 8:11)

Paul's statement is a key evidence of Christianity. There is a progressive freedom that we experience in our bodies moving away from the control of the sinful nature towards control of the Spirit. Our body experiences this as we live more and more in sync with the Spirit than in conflict with the old nature.

My body is given a new life, literally, to live in freedom from slavery of my old nature. My body not only experiences communion, communication, and companionship with God, but also experiences freedom from the bondage of sin. Subsequent to spiritual rebirth, this is one of the most incredible miracles of biblical Christianity, which every person born of the Spirit is privileged to experience.

The consequence of the transformation of the spirit, mind, and body is holiness, which is:

+ An amazing experience that aligns the new nature in us to the divine nature of God
+ Experiencing the original design
+ Being whole in character alignment with God
+ The nature of God and the nature of humanity aligned in unity
+ The mind of humanity in perfect alignment with the Spirit of God
+ Experiencing overcoming temptations
+ Living an overcoming lifestyle

THE PRINCIPLE OF DEATH BIRTHING LIFE

Therefore, brothers and sisters, we have an obligation—but it is not to the flesh, to live according to it. For if you live according to the flesh, you will die; but if by the Spirit you put to death the misdeeds of the body, you will live. (Romans 8:12-13)

The methodology of overcoming the negative triggers of the body in a born-again individual is the ultimate differentiator of the relationship that the cross births. Jesus came so humanity may enjoy abundant life here on earth in the Spirit, by the Spirit, and experienced through the Spirit.

Jesus' suffering, death, and resurrection are the prototype for humanity to experience the ability to overcome by the Spirit. Jesus died so we may be born again. He rose again so we may live like Him by dying to self! Just as Jesus died once and now lives forever, we must die to ourselves daily so we may, like Him, also live forever, as Paul stated in the verses above.

While this step is simple, it feels counterintuitive. If the seed keeps its seed coat, it cannot experience life and bear fruit. The mother must allow the baby to be born to experience the relational life with her child. Nature offers countless examples of letting go of the old to experience the new. In the work world, we can't take a new job without letting go of the old one, and we can't relocate to the corner office while staying in the cubicle.

Dying to the old enables us to embrace the new. Dying to the familiar gives birth to an amazing new future. As long as we are satisfied with the status quo, we can never experience anything new in life. A healthy dissatisfaction with the present leads us to die to the old to experience the new. We are so accustomed to the old that experiencing the reality of the new is directly related to how much we desire the new.

Understanding and applying the principle of death birthing life is one of the most powerful biblical methodologies to experience the divine nature in us. There is pain during suffering and in death, but when the other side of death is an incredible experience of what we have always longed for, then the struggle becomes worth the pain. The promise of the cross of Christ is the start of an incredible awareness of the supernatural in the natural, resulting in the end of the cosmic vacuum. This alone is worth the pain of dying to the old nature so the new nature will grow.

> For if, by the trespass of the one man, death reigned through that one man, how much more will those who receive God's abundant provision of grace and of the gift of righteousness reign in life through the one man, Jesus Christ! (Romans 5:17)

Everyday life is all about motivating ourselves to persevere when the going gets tough. Meanwhile, we make tremendous sacrifices in chasing the mirage of life. How much more can we experience the divine nature when we are transformed to let go of the old to embrace the new? Twenty-first-century

Christianity has lost the power of the "how much more" referred to in the above verse. Reigning in life is not some futuristic fantasy. Paul is writing about a present experiential reality. The *basileuo en zoe* (reign in life) is what we all long to have and are searching for.

> For the joy set before him he endured the cross, scorning
> its shame, and sat down at the right hand of the throne of
> God. (Hebrews 12:2)

"The joy" set before Jesus was not the throne of God, for that belonged to Him already! This was the *basileuo en zoe*, the dominion of the life of God in mankind. Before going to the cross, Jesus told His disciples in John 14, He would come back and *all* of God through the Holy Spirit would indwell them—in the present and future. Jesus endured the cross for the joy of living in communion with humanity. To personalize this, He endured the cross so you and I can live intimately with Him. There is an experiential personal intimacy with God that the Enemy tries to keep humanity from experiencing.

The objective of Jesus is the relational destination of mankind with God. Jesus went through what He did, not to give us some happy place to live after death but to give us the greatest blessing of living in intimacy with Him while here on earth. The pain of the cross was endured so humanity may live in an experiential communion with God in alignment with His holiness. The Perfect experienced the imperfect so the imperfect can experience the Perfect. This is the disruption of life.

> For if while we were enemies we were reconciled to God
> through the death of His Son, *it is much more* [certain],
> now that we are reconciled, that we shall be saved (daily
> delivered from sin's dominion) through His [resurrection]
> life. (Romans 5:10 AMPC)

Twenty-first-century Christianity has made the word "saved" (used in the verse above) such a historical theory that the power of the present "how much more" is diluted and all but lost. The word "saved" here is *sozo*, a verb that means to "rescue and keep safe." The historical death and resurrection of Jesus is validated in the present when we are daily rescued and delivered from the dominion of sin in the present and enabled to live in companionship with the Father. The proof of biblical history is the ability to live a present lifestyle of freedom from the slavery of actions that bring guilt and shame. Knowing that dying to the old will result in living in the new creation enables us to experience the methodology of *how* Jesus lived.

> Jesus, *full of the Holy Spirit,* left the Jordan and was led by the Spirit into the wilderness, where for forty days he was tempted by the devil. (Luke 4:1–2)

> Jesus returned to Galilee in the *power of the Spirit* … (Luke 4:14)

We see Jesus, *full of the Spirit,* being led into the wilderness where He was tempted, and He returned to Galilee in the *power of the Spirit* subsequent to overcoming temptation. Between the two, Jesus demonstrated the principle of death birthing life when He died to temptation by living from the Spirit. Jesus did not overcome the Enemy to experience God. He overcame the Enemy *because* He experienced God.

Temptation is not sin. Being tempted is not sinful. Jesus Himself was tempted. Because He was God incarnate, He could consistently display the life of death birthing life. Jesus lived this truth so we may become transformed to live the same truth. Temptation is the reality check to remind us who we truly are. Dying to the old and living in the new is the present evidence of the resurrection power of Jesus operating in us.

How we handle the temptations of life is an indicator of our transformation journey. This is a progression of moving from one level of experiencing God to the next.

We are transformed to become people who can recognize temptation and then, by the Spirit, overcome. Therefore, we are transformed to overcome. We do not overcome to be transformed. This sequence is not mere semantics but actually differentiates religion from relationship.

Temptations are part of the growth process in the new creation. We are not robots living in a sanitized environment but human beings living in an environment where the enemy seeks to steal, kill, and destroy. In the original creation, humanity was tempted but lost. In the new creation, we are tempted but win.

Our new ability to choose God over the Enemy is proven in temptation. The reality of what happens in our spiritual dimension is validated not by the expressions of what we do, but by the evidence of who we are becoming. Overcoming temptation is cognitive evidence in the mind that the spiritual rebirth in the spirit is a reality.

The goal of religion, along with most all of humanity, is simply good moral behavior. The goal of relationship is experiencing God, which has the consequence of moral behavior. If moral behavior had been the chief end of Jesus, the prostitute in John 8 would have been stoned to death. In fact, Jesus would have been the first to throw a stone. But instead He created an encounter of love and mercy for the woman to experience, and then He told her to go and sin no more.

Moral reformation leads to expressions of good behavior, which makes humanity feel good but still left to search for how to fill the inner emptiness. Spiritual transformation leads to experiencing God, resulting in the filling of the cosmic vacuum inside, which in turn brings humanity to express God.

THE JOY IN SUFFERING

For us to experience a lifestyle of freedom, which is a consequence of communion, communication, and companionship with God, we need a totally different perspective on suffering. Transformation of the mind alone can birth in us this new perspective. While this book can only give an intellectual understanding of suffering, the transformation of one's mind actually enables us to experience a changed perspective.

The suffering of Jesus is predominantly ascribed to what happened to Him physically. But before He suffered in the body, Jesus suffered in the mind. Hebrews 2:18 states, "Because he himself suffered when he was tempted, he is able to help those who are being tempted." Due to Jesus' humanity, He was tempted by the Enemy even as Adam and Eve were tempted. Jesus suffered through temptation before He suffered in physical pain.

Temptation causes conflict between the old and the new nature resulting in an internal suffering. Before Jesus died on the cross and rose again, He suffered when He was tempted and had to die to temptation. But this process allowed the life of God to consistently flow in Him and through Him. The lifestyle of Jesus was one of internal suffering due to temptation, dying to temptation, and living in the Spirit, not because of the old nature versus the new nature. But our conflict in temptation is because of the conflict between our old nature and new nature.

> Jesus went out as usual to the Mount of Olives, and his disciples followed him. On reaching the place, he said to them, "Pray that you will not fall into temptation." He withdrew about a stone's throw beyond them, knelt down and prayed, "Father, if you are willing, take this cup from me; yet not my will, but yours be done." An angel from heaven appeared to him and strengthened him. And being in anguish, he prayed more earnestly, and his sweat was like drops of blood falling to the ground. (Luke 22:38–44)

> In your struggle against sin, you have not yet resisted to the point of shedding your blood. (Hebrews 12:4)

Temptation produces internal conflict and this conflict produces suffering within. Jesus resisted temptation to the point of His anguish creating the physical circumstance of sweating blood. The writer to the Hebrews is encouraging his audience to resist the lure of the flesh and the enemy, even as Jesus resisted, suffered, and overcame. Transformation leads to the mind being willing and wanting to resist, leading to an internal struggle and suffering, which leads to overcoming. A transformed mind says, "Not my will but yours be done" and it is in that moment of yielding to the Spirit that we experience resurrection power.

> For we do not have a high priest who is unable to empathize with our weaknesses, but we have one who has been tempted in every way, just as we are—yet he did not sin. (Hebrews 4:15)

Jesus was tempted in *every way* that a human can be tempted. Imagine if Adam and Eve had taken the choice to die to the lure of the Enemy and refuse his temptation in the garden. The result would have been a life spent in the original dimension for eternity where time and space do not exist! Imagine then, subsequent to repentance and belief, we choose to suffer and die to the lure of the Enemy and refuse his temptations. The result would be the incredible resurrection life of Jesus experienced in and through us. The journey of transformation subsequent to repentance and belief enables the experience of this incredible resurrection power.

The Christian journey is a simple choice to suffer the conflicts of temptation and die to self, which leads to the incredible life of God bursting in and from us. This choice to suffer temptation is directly related to the transformation of the mind. The Spirit of God takes the Word of God and transforms the mind of the individual to the mind of Christ so that just as Christ made the choice to listen and abide by the Spirit, we too will make the choice to deny the old nature and live by the new nature.

We may not like this constant dilemma, but we cannot escape it. Twenty-first-century Christianity teaches that all suffering always comes from an external source. But we must understand the internal as well. Unless we first handle the internal suffering caused by the sinful desires that war within us, we will never be able to handle external sufferings.

> Therefore, since we have been justified through faith, we have peace with God through our Lord Jesus Christ, through whom we have gained access by faith into this grace in which we now stand. And we boast in the hope of the glory of God. Not only so, but we also glory in our sufferings, because we know that suffering produces perseverance; perseverance, character; and character, hope. (Romans 5:1–4)

Today, we like the concepts of justification, peace with God, access to faith, and the hope of glory, but Paul continues on to say we "glory in our suffering" too. Is this some kind of self-destructive perspective? How can we glory in suffering? How did Paul do this? His life was one of continual internal and external suffering, and yet he always rejoiced in hope.

He wrote that suffering produces perseverance, character, and hope. He encourages the Romans to embrace the suffering of overcoming temptation, to choose to die when temptations occur. This will then teach them to persevere and gain victory over sin that produces character and builds hope.

The greatest hope that humanity can have is a future of perfection evidenced by the present experiential reality of God and humanity in communion, communication, and companionship. This present internal and experiential reality gives us hope for an incredible future. The suffering of temptation and overcoming by the Spirit becomes joy when we know the end result is an experiential awareness of God that brings us real hope in this life.

The greatest miracle that humanity needs to experience is that of living a life of holiness in communion, communication, and companionship with God. The greatest miracle that humanity needs to experience is the miracle of being enabled to not do what we do not want to do. The suffering that Western Christians need to face today is in fighting the war that is raging within ourselves. There are far too many fighting the moral wars of the world, when, personally, they have lost the war to live an overcoming life with God.

We have a hopeless brand of Christianity when we have a theoretical faith without practical character formation. Christians live hopeless lives when they do not see the evidence of God through growing in godly character. When we do not experience *holiness*, we have *hopelessness*. Therefore, hopelessness is a direct result of lacking character. Lacking character is a direct result of lacking perseverance. Lacking perseverance is a direct result of refusing to suffer internal conflict. Living an overcoming life is one of the internal evidences of sonship identity.

THE CORRELATION BETWEEN SUFFERING AND WORSHIP

The word *worship*, like so many other English words in this century, has become convoluted in its meaning. In today's Christian circles, worship means singing songs with lyrics about God to melodies that elevate an emotional state. This has become an event where the more positive the emotions felt, the closer the association assumed with God. The higher the feeling, the greater the "presence" of God is felt. The best barometer to differentiate emotions from spirituality is what happens *after* the worship time during the week. If the feeling goes away, it is most likely the hormones that were triggered during the "worship" time!

The words *aboda* (Hebrew, also *abad* or *asab*) and *latreia* (Greek, also *latreuo*) are frequently translated as *worship*. In the Old Testament, these words typically refer to service associated with work done in the temple. Thus, the term *latreia* and its derivatives are directly associated with service and sacrifice directed toward God.

Other terms are translated as *worship*, including the Greek word *proskyneo* and its Hebrew equivalent, *shachac*. Both terms refer to a posture of submission and thus an acknowledgment of God's sovereignty. This is evident in the word pictures of bending the knee (*gonu* or *gonupeteo*), bowing down (*histahawa*, or the Hebrew *shachac*), or of *proskyneo* ("to kiss forward" in Greek).

> Therefore, I urge you, brothers and sisters, in view of God's mercy, to offer your bodies as a living sacrifice, holy and pleasing to God—this is your true and proper worship. (Romans 12:1)

True worship is offering our bodies as living sacrifices. Biblical worship as explained in the New Testament is not musical but transformational! We face great deception when we think that singing emotionally charged songs fulfills our requirements of worship. The enemy has fooled a generation into deception by connecting worship solely to music and songs.

There is no greater worship that is pleasing to God than a person living as a sacrifice. Even going to the Third World as a missionary is not as great a sacrifice as dying to the triggers of the body and living by the Spirit. Biblical worship is the choice that we make every moment to die to ourselves and live by the leading of the Spirit. When God told Abraham to sacrifice his son, He appeared to be making a brutal request. In fact, this was a profound act of love, foreshadowing Jesus' suffering, sacrificial death, and resurrection. As Abraham made the choice of death, he experienced the greatest life.

Daniel was tempted to follow the law of the land, but he chose to die, literally, but then he lived. Joseph was tempted into an adulterous situation and chose to die to the lure of the woman, but then he lived. Queen Esther was tempted to not give up the luxury of the palace and chose to die, literally, and not only did she live, but her nation was spared as well.

As Abraham laid the body of Isaac on the altar of sacrifice in worship to God, we lay our bodies as a living sacrifice, choosing to die by the Spirit so we will live. This is worship in Spirit and in truth. An hour a week in an emotionally elevated state of being called worship is one of the greatest deceptions today in the religion called Christianity. We must separate praise from worship. Worship is a 24/7 lifestyle sacrificing our old nature to live in the new.

Transformation of the mind makes Romans 12 "true and proper worship" an experiential reality. When there is no worship resulting from death birthing life Monday through Saturday in our everyday realities, this becomes religion to go through an emotional or intellectual worship on Sundays.

THE HUMAN BODY: THE TEMPLE OF GOD

A relationship with God happens in us because we become the temple of God. Our body becomes the residence of God. This is not a belief statement or a spiritual declaration, but a real-life experience.

Experiencing and enjoying God in us, which we were meant to do, and being His children through His Spirit is worth every moment of suffering as we die to the old nature and its desires. The Enemy keeps telling us the old nature's actions and activities are better, but you and I will realize that the new spiritual experience with God Himself inside us is indescribable.

> Don't you know that you yourselves are God's temple and that God's Spirit dwells in your midst? (1 Corinthians 3:16)

> For we are the temple of the living God. As God has said: "I will live with them and walk among them, and I will be their God, and they will be my people." (2 Corinthians 6:16)

From the time God revealed Himself on Mount Sinai, to His coming and dwelling in the tent among the Israelites, to His dwelling in the Holy of Holies in the temple, and finally to His dwelling in us, God has been in pursuit of humanity for a relationship of communion, communication, and companionship. Through the cross of Christ, God has set up a Holy of Holies in each of us where we can meet Him. This *sanctum sanctorum* gives us what we long for—a meeting with God in intimate communion. This is available 24/7 regardless of circumstances, an inner constant that defines all external variables.

When we wake up in the morning and the reality of life bears down on us, we can experience the Holy of Holies inside us. This puts into perspective all that we might face. Our minds are embraced by God Himself. There are no words in any human language that can articulate this inner reality of the embrace of God cognitively experienced by our mind.

> "And now, compelled by the Spirit, I am going to Jerusalem, not knowing what will happen to me there. I only know that in every city the Holy Spirit warns me that prison and hardships are facing me." (Acts 20:22–23)

Paul is at peace about going to Jerusalem because of the incredible rest He finds in the Person of God. In fact, this experience inside him was of greater importance to Paul than the potentially dangerous physical consequences. His inner awareness of God was so strong and real that what happened to his body became inconsequential. This is the state of the martyr. The inner witness is so strong that they are willing to lose their lives. We will live lives that matter when Jesus Himself who died for us all leads our journey of transformation. The reality of the joy of God will draw us away from the reality of the destructive desires that war within us. In the midst of extreme success, in the midst of fear of loss or even absolute loss, the reality of the Temple of God inside us will burst into experience.

The body of mankind becomes the place of God in communion and communication as we hear Him in this inner temple. The immortal spiritual dimension in mankind becomes the temple of God.

COSMIC WARFARE

When we are adopted into being children of God, we enter a cosmic warzone. The objective of the Enemy is to steal, kill, and destroy the children of the King.

The Enemy devises his strategy to achieve his objectives on three levels:

1—DECEPTION

He works to have people separate the experience of grace from expressing grace. This confuses people into thinking they are bound for Heaven when they are actually only members of the religion called Christianity.

2—DISTRACTION

He works to have people lose the war on ungodliness and get so focused on defining their identity by what they do, not by who they are becoming. The result is hectic human activity with no godly effects.

3—DIVISION

He works to get people to fight among themselves through denominational and interpersonal divisions where diversity is not practiced and uniformity is demanded.

Deception keeps people in the dark.

Distraction keeps people inwardly focused.

Division keeps people from reflecting God's image and glory.

The Enemy will do anything—*anything*—to ensure that people do not become like Jesus. He wants to keep people focused on acting like Jesus as long as they won't be like Jesus!

The book of Job gives us great insight as to the cause in the supernatural dimension and its effect in the natural dimension.

> Then the Lord said to Satan, "Have you considered my servant Job? There is no one on earth like him; he is

blameless and upright, a man who fears God and shuns evil." (Job 1:8)

God focuses on the being of Job that "fears God and shuns evil." If there is no internal fear of God, there can be no external shunning of evil.

"Does Job fear God for nothing?" Satan replied. "Have you not put a hedge around him and his household and everything he has? You have blessed the work of his hands, so that his flocks and herds are spread throughout the land. But now stretch out your hand and strike everything he has, and he will surely curse you to your face." (Job 1:9–11)

The Enemy responds to God by saying Job's being is only because of his doing—all his wealth and possessions—and if God removed what he has, Job would walk away from Him.

When our identity of being a child of God is derived from what we have and what we do, which are variables, when these are removed or when they change, our fundamental identity gets challenged and shaken. When Jesus is presented only as a Miracle Worker, then the foundations of faith are shaken when the miraculous does not come our way. When Jesus is presented as a wealth and health Provider, the foundations of faith are shaken when wealth and health don't come or are taken away.

But when the Enemy strips away everything that Job has, then:

At this, Job got up and tore his robe and shaved his head. Then he fell to the ground in worship and said: "Naked I came from my mother's womb, and naked I will depart. The Lord gave and the Lord has taken away; may the name of the Lord be praised." (Job 1:20–21)

When Job's wife gave up on him, this is how he responds:

His wife said to him, "Are you still maintaining your integrity? Curse God and die!" He replied, "You are talking like a foolish woman. Shall we accept good from God, and

not trouble?" In all this, Job did not sin in what he said.
(Job 2:9–10)

The Person of God supersedes the provisions of God. The inner constant defines the external variable. His spiritual identity defined Job's physical identity. Job's *being* defined Job's *doing* (his possessions). Job won the cosmic war because his identity was never defined by what he did or by what God did but by the Person of God. What differentiates the winners from the losers in this cosmic warzone is their focus is on the Person of Christ, staying with Jesus, transforming to become like Jesus, and having His mind, therefore overcoming like Christ.

Prayer: Practicing the Presence of the Father

In Matthew 6, Jesus taught His disciples to pray, starting off by saying, "Our Father in heaven."

> Very early in the morning, while it was still dark, Jesus got up, left the house and went off to a solitary place, where he prayed. (Mark 1:35)

While prayer was a regular and continual practice for Him, we see in multiple places in Scripture how Jesus made this His focus. This was a very private time of intimacy with the Father. This is how we become more and more aware of the Father God. This is when we hear the Father say, "You are my child." This is where all theory becomes reality. This is not consciousness, not sub-consciousness, not positive thinking, and not the power of positive words. Prayer is the inter-dimensional communion, communication, and companionship between God and mankind.

As we grow in our cognitive awareness of God, we will realize that our sensitivity to the Spirit increases, as well as an inner conscious 24/7 awareness of God. For the majority of our lives, we are not aware of our own breathing. As much as breathing is natural to us, the inner awareness of God becomes just as natural. Prayer becomes an inner constant of communication with God. Religion teaches us all about the discipline of prayer, which is why so many eventually give up on a regular meeting time with God. A relationship can still have all the disciplines but the focus is always communing with the Father first. While I may set certain dates or times with my wife and family for specific talks and fellowship, my relationship with them draws me to have constant interaction and communication to grow in intimacy.

We must be careful to not designate places where we "feel" God. We must remind ourselves that spirituality is very different from emotion. As we grow in our inner awareness of God, as we *ginosko* (know) Him, we will be talking to our Father continually, constantly. There is conscious communion, communication, and companionship—*all* the time. This life with Him is beautiful and incredibly awesome. My children do not always need to know how I am going to navigate our family through the good and bad circumstances of life. All they need to know is that Dad is there. My *presence* is of far greater importance than my *presents*.

Prayer is an incredible time when we experience the Person of God beyond our thoughts, feelings, and emotions. The Person of God becomes a reality where He empowers us to overcome our present condition. Whether in the midst of plenty or poverty, there is an inner awareness of God that fills us. When the fear of the future grips us in the midst of so many political and economic variables, there is a literal embrace of the Father in the midst of that emotion of fear. When the joy of great achievement wanes away, there is a literal whisper of the Father that He is the purpose of life!

Prayer is the Person of God gripping a person in the inner realms beyond the mind and body. This does not require any external stimuli. In the midst of the most painful situations in life, the Person of God overrides and becomes an inner Rock. This is an experience available for all of humanity, what we long and hope for in our innermost being—a Person *inside* us who is *with* us in spite of what *happens* to us. Then and only then will what happens to us not define who we are because of who is in us.

EXPERIENCING PERSONAL IDENTITY: THE PERSON-DRIVEN LIFE

Purpose in life is integral to who we are as humans. We live in an extremely purpose-driven culture. But we can move from success to significance in life by changing what we *do*. I know people who stopped driving downtown to pursue the corporate dream and now instead go to the inner city to feed the poor and educate the underprivileged. But regardless of the destination, the person's identity is defined by the purpose of what is done and achieved. The cosmic vacuum continues to haunt the inner being, irrespective of all the good that is done. The new creation of God repurposes the meaning of purpose. In the new creation, we feed the poor and educate the underprivileged because of who we have become and not to define whom we are. Being births doing. Doing does not and cannot define being.

Moving from a purpose-driven life to a Person-driven life involves the transition from religion to relationship. As we progress through the methodology of the new creation and experience the overcoming lifestyle, as we experience our identity as children of God, the consequence is the incredible purpose we experience. Our purpose is not to glorify God here on earth. Our purpose is to live in a relationship of communion with the God of all glory. Our purpose supersedes the promise, prophecy, and provisions of God to the very Person of God. The purpose of life is to regain the original design of living in an experiential relationship with God through transformation of the mind by the Spirit of God by the Word of God.

Religion forces us to glorify God on earth by what we do, while relationship transforms us to become like the God of all glory. His glory will then flow through us. We can either focus on the *glory* of God or we can focus on the *God* of glory. We live a purpose-driven life when we seek to glorify God. We live a Person-driven life when the God of glory makes His dwelling in us and we experience communion, communication, and companionship with the God of all glory. In the former, the "I" is in control; in the latter, Jesus is in control. This is what separates the religion called Christianity from the relationship to which Jesus calls us.

Living in this Father-and-child relationship is our primary purpose in life. The Enemy keeps trying to convince us the purpose of a Christian is what we do for God and what God does through us. This is the Devil's lie. There can be no other purpose but God Himself. Our ultimate purpose is experiencing the power of God at work as He transforms us into the image of Christ so we again experience our original personal identity as a child of God. No matter how great our accomplishments for God might be, this will never create purpose. God is not a purpose-giver; He is a Life-Giver.

David was one of Israel's greatest leaders. As a shepherd boy, he was anointed as the future king. The prophet Samuel spoke about God's purpose for David. If David were purpose-driven, he would have killed Saul at the first opportunity. But David was Person-driven and Spirit-controlled, so he did not act on his own. David was totally secure in his personal identity of who he was and who God was to him. Therefore, God fulfilled His purpose through David. God's plan was for David to follow Him, experience Him, and delight in Him. When David experienced personal identity and lived out his relational identity with God, then God's purpose through David was fulfilled as a consequence (1 Samuel 16).

David received the blueprint for the temple from God. He had access to wealth, so the next logical step would have been to build the temple to fulfill God's plan (2 Samuel 7). If David were purpose-driven, he would have forged ahead and built the temple. What a legacy he could have left behind! Doesn't this make sense to our twenty-first-century minds? But when God is our purpose in life, we do what He wants, not what we believe is right for Him. If He is our God, then He is a constant. What God does through us is the variable.

Moses started his life as purpose-driven. Though he grew up in the king's palace, his mother knew his identity as the deliverer of his people. The first time he had to take sides, he protected his people and killed an Egyptian. What Moses did was an expression of his identity and purpose— Israelite first and deliverer second. Eventually, the mandate for Moses was clear: take God's people to the Promised Land.

On the way, the Israelites disobeyed God many times, so He became angry and told Moses, "Leave this place, you and the people you brought up out of Egypt, and go up to the land I promised on oath to Abraham, Isaac and Jacob, saying, 'I will give it to your descendants.' I will send an angel before you and drive out the Canaanites, Amorites, Hittites, Perizzites, Hivites and Jebusites. Go up to the land flowing with milk and honey. But I will not go with you, because you are a stiff-necked people and I might destroy you on the way" (Exodus 33:1–3).

If Moses were purpose-driven and if he were a twenty-first-century Christian, he would have naturally responded, "That's fine, God. Thanks for coming with us up to this point. From now on, we can handle it. We know what to do, and we can fight our way into the land." And then he would have uttered the iconic twenty-first-century phrase: "Don't worry. We got this!"

But Moses had an experiential relationship with God.

> Then Moses said to him, "If your Presence does not go with
> us, do not send us up from here. How will anyone know
> that you are pleased with me and with your people unless
> you go with us? What else will distinguish me and your
> people from all the other people on the face of the earth?"
> (Exodus 33:15–16)

A purpose-driven man was transformed into a Person-driven man. The differentiating factor for Moses was not the miracle of manna but the Person of God in the Israelites' midst. Moses did not care about God's special effects. Moses was not about the glory of God but about the God of all glory. He was passionate about who God was. This is the power of spiritual transformation.

Twenty-first-century Christianity teaches us to act like Moses, while biblical Christianity transforms us to be like Moses. When we experience a Spirit-to-spirit communion with God, we move from being purpose-driven to Person-driven.

When we experience the Person of God, we experience our identity as a child of God and consequentially we experience the purpose of God for us. Purpose is a consequence of knowing the Person and living in an experiential relationship of communion, communication, and companionship with the Person, Jesus Christ. The purpose of humanity is to experience the Person called Jesus Christ.

EXPERIENCING PRIVILEGE IDENTITY:
THE PURPOSE OF GOD THROUGH US

Religion makes us focus on a purpose to do and achieve for God, while relationship enables us to experience God as the purpose. Good intentions of purpose that humans have to do for God are not God-intended purposes in us.

May these be the words said about us: "Now when David had served God's purpose in his own generation, he fell asleep" (Acts 13:36).

God is raising up a generation that is Person-driven, that experiences a sonship identity, and that, as a consequence, accomplishes the purpose of God, not *their* purpose for God.

In the new creation as we walk the transformational journey, God's purpose through us is accomplished. God's purpose in us is the cause; God's purpose through us is the effect. Personal identity is the cause; privilege identity is the consequence.

This sequence is important because one of the temptations of a child of God is to confuse personal identity with privilege identity, the same dilemma that Adam and Eve faced. Our desire for name and fame begins to distort our personal identity in being children of God and we begin to act like little gods.

When privilege identity supersedes personal identity, we create idols, we become idols, and what started as a movement of God can become a monument for God. But when our purpose is the Person of God, we would say as Jesus told us in Luke 17:10, "So you also, when you have done everything you were told to do, should say, 'We are unworthy servants; we have only done our duty.'"

This order ensures that blessings do not turn into curses. How many children of God started off on the right path, experiencing sonship identity, with privileges pouring into their lives, only to have their eyes move away from the Person to the privileges and then lives are destroyed or religious systems are created. But when the purpose of mankind is the Person of God, privileges do not consume us.

> For God, who said, "Let light shine out of darkness," made his light shine in our hearts to give us the light of the knowledge of God's glory displayed in the face of Christ. But we have this treasure in jars of clay to show that this all-surpassing power is from God and not from us." (2 Corinthians 4:6–7)

When our purpose is the Person of God, we will realize we are vessels of clay that carry the all-surpassing power of God. Personal identity would so consume us that we would not be carried away by the privileges that God gives to us. That internal spiritual communion, communication, and companionship with God would be so real and incredibly amazing that we would not be influenced but enabled and empowered to deny the lure of the mind and body to glory in His privileges. When we experience the best as an internal constant, why would we go for the inferior, which is an external variable? God is in us and what He does in us is a constant; what God does through us is a variable.

> Then Jesus came to them and said, "All authority in heaven and on earth has been given to me. Therefore go and make disciples of all nations, baptizing them in the name of the Father and of the Son and of the Holy Spirit, and teaching them to obey everything I have commanded you. And surely I am with you always, to the very end of the age." (Matthew 28:18–20)

Various promotional models today exist centered around this command of Jesus. As we have seen before, discipleship comes through spending time with Him. In this passage, He is telling His disciples to bring in more people to live life and spend time with Him. Making disciples is not a job description to fulfill but a lifestyle to follow. When we live the lifestyle of discipleship in our personal lives, we will make disciples in the community. Religion tells us to go and make disciples as a job, agenda, and vocation. Relationship enables us to become disciples as a lifestyle that in turn makes other disciples.

"Go and make disciples" is a command of Jesus found in Matthew 28, but the methodology of making disciples differentiates between religion and relationship. The former is a legalistic command to obey, while the latter is a relationship of love that overflows. Jesus did not say in Matthew 4 that He would teach people how to fish for men. He said, "I will *make* you fishers of men." Being made to be like Jesus is an incredible experience compared to imitating what Jesus did. When we are made to be like Jesus, the same compassion that made Him do what He did will also overwhelm us to do the same! When doing comes as a compassionate overflow from who we are being and becoming, it is an incredible place of freedom and liberation, and where God works through us. There is no "spiritual burnout" here.

All humanity is in a constant process of "evangelizing and witnessing."

That is how our favorite products, services, and entertainment are promoted. We experience and we share what we experience. The command of Jesus to make disciples is the same. We become disciples who make disciples. This is not a job or vocation but is the basic fabric of human nature. There are no part-time disciples.

In the early church, global missions were conducted through a methodology of kingdom people living out this kingdom lifestyle with the consequence being the kingdom of God established. When we make evangelism and missions into a strategy done only as a vocation, then no matter how great the mission work is, this becomes a religious model to promote personal and organizational agendas.

God is raising up a generation of salt and light where the kingdom lifestyle is not what is done but a lifestyle of love that is lived out (Matthew 5:13-14). In the early church, when the gospel spread as persecution broke out, people were scattered, and as they lived out their personal identity, people witnessed Jesus in them. Consequentially, people witnessed Jesus through them.

The gospel spread in the early years when people took their vocation and went to foreign lands. Who they were and what they did was so tightly integrated that whether they made tents, herded sheep, or worked with wood, they were salt and light in their communities. In the last few decades, well-intentioned people made evangelism into a full-time vocation, leaving the majority of the people in the church with little to no opportunity to be witnesses.

> "But you will receive power when the Holy Spirit comes on you; and you will *be* my witnesses in Jerusalem, and in all Judea and Samaria, and to the ends of the earth." (Acts 1:8)

Jesus did not tell His disciples to "do" witnessing. He made a statement of fact that the Holy Spirit would come and they would *be* His witnesses. The Spirit of God coming was the *cause*, and being a witness was a *consequence*. When the Spirit of God came, they witnessed God within them. When they witnessed God in them, they became like the God in them and people saw God through them. When they lived as disciples, witnessing was not what they did but a life they lived, and others witnessed God in them.

When we witness Jesus in us, the world will witness Jesus through us as a consequence. When the world witnesses Jesus through us, God's purpose is fulfilled.

It is totally against biblical principles that we can fulfill God's purpose in China but not in our own lives, for our families, or our neighbors. The Enemy has lured us into accepting this fallacy and deception. We think that our purpose in life is to send someone a check, and then this act absolves us from being witnesses right where we are. Christian ministry is not what we do but a consequence of who we become. This begins at home, in our communities and work places where people experience unconditional love. Religion makes ministry into a church organizational program. Relationship makes ministry a lifestyle.

An excuse we often use is, "Peter was called. Stephen was called. Paul was called. But not me." We have just as much of a calling from God as Paul, Peter, or any of the other disciples. Having a calling is a biblical principle that does not exclude any child of God from living out their identity. In fact, they *will* live their identity as a principle of life.

We learn to say, for example, "I am not gifted in evangelism." Gifting is a biblical principle that does not exclude any child of God from living out their identity. Being a new creation as a child of God is an experiential identity that we will express irrespective of circumstances and locations. It is a twenty-first-century contradiction to make the claim of Christian identity and then live a lifestyle that is contrary to Christ. Living the Jesus life—wherever we are—is the calling for every Christian.

All the people in the Bible are prototypes of the Person of God in how they came into their purpose, thereby God accomplishing His will on earth. When they lived in their communion, communication, and companionship with God, the purpose of God was fulfilled. Inter-dimensional communication was the cause, while the purpose of God accomplished was the effect. Experiencing personal identity is the cause, while the expression of privilege identity is the consequence.

There is an incredible all-surpassing power that God wants to demonstrate in this day and age, the privilege of being a vessel of love in a generation that is seeking love. Being people who experience the God of love and so express the love of God is the deep need of our time. Being a person of love who lives above race, religion, denomination, and geography is what the world desperately longs to see. The cross of Christ is still the answer to the greatest needs in the world today.

Choose Life!

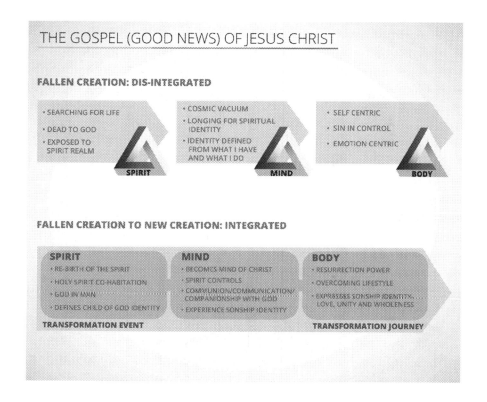

In the fallen creation, we can choose destruction and death while knowing the consequences. The choice involving God has mystified and confused humanity throughout the ages. But when we change our minds about the God of the Christian Scriptures, believing in Jesus and His finished work on the cross, we set in motion a journey of transformational relationship with God and return to who we were always meant to be.

God does not force us to love Him. He awaits our choice, desiring an obliging love, not an obligatory love. God seeks after us but behaves as the waiting Lover. He has done His part with the cross being the visible expression of His love. He now wants us to respond with the action of choice. All the circumstances of life, the good and the bad, prompt us to choose the life of God, start a relationship to discover His Father's heart, and experience His great love.

> Therefore, my dear friends, as you have always obeyed—not only in my presence, but now much more in my absence—continue to *work* out your salvation with fear and trembling, for it is God who *works* in you to will and to act in order to fulfill his good purpose. (Philippians 2:12–13)

Human beings are called to repent and believe, resulting in the miracle of the rebirth of the spirit of the individual and the cohabitation of the Spirit of God. The Word of God transforms our mind to the mind of Christ and our mind embraces the death birthing life principle that takes us deeper and deeper into this journey of knowing and experiencing the Person of God. There is an incredible work of humanity and work of God that takes us on this relational journey. There is one original creation principle that continues into the fallen and the new creation of humanity, and that is the power of choice.

Choice is one constant that does not change in humanity. While the hope is that this book would push you toward the awesomeness of having a spiritual relationship with God, the choice remains only with you. God would not override that choice. While He desires all humanity to be saved and live in a spiritual relationship with Him, it is a choice that an individual needs to make.

We do not and cannot choose to save ourselves. That is religion. We choose to change our mind about Jesus and believe what He accomplished on the cross. When we make that choice, God starts working in us to rebirth our spirit, co-inhabit in us through His Holy Spirit, and start this incredible journey of making the reality of the Spirit a cognitive experience expressed through the body.

We cannot transform ourselves any more than a caterpillar can transform itself into a butterfly. All the caterpillar does is eat and rest. All we are called to do is read the Word. The Word of God transforms the mind of mankind to experience the mind of Christ to think differently and choose to suffer and die so we may live. Like a butterfly, we begin to let go of the old to experience the new. This is the miracle of life that Jesus offers.

I can articulate this to you but cannot make it happen for you. God works in you to make it happen. Our role is to choose the eternal life of God who is a Person, and His name is Jesus Christ.

Maybe you are at the stage of life where all we have shared thus far still does not make sense. You are not ready to make that choice. Would you pray that you might one day want to make the choice? The awesomeness of God is that you can let Him know that you want the desire to want to choose Him.

If the message of this book makes sense to you but you do not want to make the choice now, then pray that you will want to choose. Say something like, "I am unable to leave my old ways, but I want to, so help me." This prayer sounds sweet to God. There is no pretense with Jesus. All He seeks is an honest human being seeking Him for who He is. All the arguments against the historical evidence of Jesus will change when the Person of Christ becomes a present reality through the simple act of choosing to repent and believe.

MEASUREMENT OF THE NEW CREATION

All religions have measurements to evaluate whether people are following its rules and adhering to its principles. Defining Christianity by what we do is extremely dangerous because it is possible to do the works of Christ without Christ! This is the pride and power of religion.

This is how we measure our spirituality:

+ You attend ten programs and I attend one.
+ You give a thousand dollars and I give a hundred.
+ You are the worship leader and I am the usher.
+ You are the pastor and I am the parishioner.
+ You are onstage and I am backstage.
+ You are the motivator and I am the one in need of ministry.
+ You are the author and I am the reader.

Church attendance has become the single greatest spiritual measurement of twenty-first-century Christianity. Participation in church activities is the strongest spiritual measure we have today. If you are a pastor, missionary, or other recognized leader, you go to an entirely different level. If you are affiliated with a mega-church, you have had the ultimate success. The Pharisees of Jesus' time had measurements much like these that showed what they did externally and demonstrated to everyone around them just how "godly" they were.

So is it even a biblical principle to measure our spiritual growth?

> Examine yourselves to see whether you are in the faith; test yourselves. Do you not realize that Christ Jesus is in you—unless, of course, you fail the test? (2 Corinthians 13:5)

The Greek word *peirazo* means "examine." *Pistis* means "faith." *Dokimazo* means "test," especially to ascertain if the local currency is fake or legitimate. *Adokimos* means "fail the test."

Paul is asking the Corinthians to examine themselves to see if their faith is original or counterfeit. Religion fools us into false affirmations of our identity, while a relationship with Jesus can be tested and proven. In 1 Peter 1:7 and James 1:3, the apostles also recommend testing the falsity or the originality of faith.

We test everything in life. We measure health, wealth, intelligence, and corporate success. But we convince ourselves that spirituality should not and cannot be tested or measured.

However, Paul is not asking Christians to test one another but to test themselves. This is not meant to be a social competition but a personal evaluation. This is not about judgment or condemnation. When we understand examining and testing from the perspective of personal measurement and evaluation, this becomes easier, bringing value and meaning to the measurement. The present and eternal consequences are far too great to ignore such testing to see if we are indeed in the religion called Christianity or if we are in the transformational journey of a relationship.

When I measured my spirituality and the evidence of life inside me compared with the measurements of the Bible, I realized that I was far, far away from being in an authentic relationship with Christ. In fact, this book is simply a product of my journey as a Christian who finally discovered the meaning of being in a relationship with Christ. Evidence does not always lead to belief, but believing in Jesus will *always* lead to His evidence.

The book of 1 John centers around one single theme, "This is how we know we are in him." John explicitly outlines the measurements or benchmarks of an authentic relationship with Jesus, such as knowing that we have passed from death to life, because we love each other and understanding that anyone who does not love remains in death. The external expression of the internal evidence of moving from death to life is love! Biblically, hate and Hell go together, love and life go together. Where there is hate, there is no life. We can have love without life but can never have hate if we have Christ's life!

Measurement 1: Child-of-God Identity

+ What is the basis of my claim to be called a Christian? Is it a historical event or a present relational and transformational journey?
+ Is my Christian identity defined by what I do on the outside or into who I am becoming transformed on the inside? What are the evidences of my transformation?
+ If every *thing* that I have is stripped away—money, position, possessions, job, and ministry, would I be at rest in my inner being from simply knowing the Person of Jesus?
+ Does the law of the land define my expression of Christian identity?
+ Do I selectively reveal and hide my Christian identity?
+ Do I follow God for who He is or for what He gives?
+ Do I experience an inner constant in the midst of external variables?
+ Is the source of my joy and confidence derived from spiritual, intellectual, and physical accomplishments?
+ Do I blame the immaturity of my Christian growth on my poor experience and expression of the fruit of the Spirit?
+ Would I consider myself to be dead spiritually if I am immature year after year without experiencing character transformation with little or no fruit?

- Am I aware of the Spirit-to-spirit testimony that defines my identity as a child of God?

MEASUREMENT 2: MORAL COMPASS

- Who am I in my private life, and who am I in public?
- Is the gap between my inside and outside progressively narrowing or widening?
- Is my external expression a reflection of my internal experience?
- Do I have a secret life in which sin is accepted, practiced, and enjoyed with no grief?
- Is there an area of my life where I won't stop sin, not because I cannot but because I don't want to?
- Can I choose not to sin even when no one would ever find out about it?

MEASUREMENT 3: SOCIAL COMPASS—LOVE

- What in my life reflects my love for other Christians?
- When people engage with me, do they experience Christ's love?
- Is there evidence that I unconditionally love the world as Jesus did?
- Do I selectively decide whom I will love?
- Are there people who I hate?
- Are there people who I refuse to love?
- How many people with value systems different from mine would call me a friend? (List the names of people who will call you a friend who do not accept your belief system.)
- Is my relationship with others based on race, color of skin, religion, denominations, or geography? (List the names of people who will call you friend who do not belong to your community, religion, race, language, or culture.)
- Where is the evidence that I unconditionally love the people in the body of Christ?

+ Where is the evidence that I unconditionally love my spouse and my children?
+ Does my family experience Jesus inside my home?
+ Do my coworkers experience Jesus around me in the workplace?
+ Do I relate to people and judge them solely by what they do and have?

MEASUREMENT 4: SOCIAL COMPASS—UNITY

+ Are my religious relationships filtered through skin color, religion, geographical boundaries, denominational barriers, and theological differences?
+ Where is the evidence that I regularly cross these divisive barriers?
+ Does my political ideology get confused and conflict with my Christian identity so that I view people through two different lenses?
+ How is my relationship with people who are not part of my denomination?

Part V
Future Creation

"What no eye has seen, what no ear has heard, and what no human mind has conceived"—the things God has prepared for those who love him—these are the things God has revealed to us by his Spirit. (1 Corinthians 2:9–10)

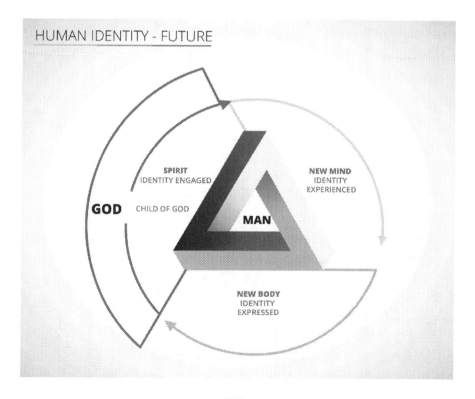

HUMAN IDENTITY - FUTURE

SPIRIT
IDENTITY ENGAGED

NEW MIND
IDENTITY
EXPERIENCED

GOD   CHILD OF GOD

MAN

NEW BODY
IDENTITY
EXPRESSED

The Truth About Death

Human identity as children of God started with the original creation, was broken in the fallen creation, and is reborn in the new creation, complete with a final destination in the future creation.

The final destination is life with God without the limitations of sin, sinful nature, sinful desires, and temptations. Christian or not, we consider death the final destination of life. We do not view death as the beginning of a new life. We think death brings life to an abrupt end. We then move into some sort of futuristic fantasy, depending on personal belief.

But there is a beautiful connection between the life we now live and the life we will live after death. Conception in our mothers is the starting point of our spiritual lives, while physical birth is the starting point of our lives on earth. Spiritual re-birth is the starting point of eternity while here on earth. Physical death is the transition point for humanity from the physical dimension into the supernatural dimension. From conception to eternity, life is one single continuum. Physical time on earth is bound by time and space. Eternity is not bound by either death or time. The utopian dreams of today are the reality of the future creation. We will be in the dimension of the ever-present where now it is not even possible to grasp the implication of living outside time and space.

Imagine a life where there is no suffering, pain, wars, discrimination, or poverty; where there is no yesterday or tomorrow and we live in the incredible dimension of the ever-present. Here we can achieve incredible success and are not defined by it. While it is certainly quite difficult for the human mind to comprehend these heavenly qualities here and now, the reality is these are fully available in the dimension of the future creation for those who live in communion, communication, and companionship with God in the present.

What occurs after physical death seems to be such a fantasy that we are unable to connect the present to the future or bring the relevance of the future into the present. If our new creation identity lived out today as children of God does not have connection to the identity we will have after death, then the present will not affect the future. But when we experience the fallen creation transitioned into the new creation, the future creation becomes a transition into a new dimension, a journey we started at the cross of Christ.

THE FUTURE STARTS HERE AND NOW

> But when the set time had fully come, God sent his Son, born of a woman, born under the law, to redeem those under the law, that we might receive adoption to sonship. Because you are his sons, God sent the Spirit of his Son into our hearts, the Spirit who calls out, "Abba, Father." So you are no longer a slave, but God's child; and since you are his child, God has made you also an heir. (Galatians 4:4–7)

The future creation is a relational inheritance for humanity. Heaven is for the sons and daughters of God who chose that identity while on earth. This identity is the starting point for the future creation. The realm of the spirit will become the epicenter of our bodies, and we will live from the spirit alone. Other than this, there will be no surprises in the transition from the dimension of the new creation to the dimension of the future creation. Unfortunately, for those who claim to be carrying an identity as children of God but are presently living lifestyles that contradict that claim, there is only bad news.

> "Not everyone who says to me, 'Lord, Lord,' will enter the kingdom of heaven, but only the one who does the will of my Father who is in heaven. Many will say to me on that day, 'Lord, Lord, did we not prophesy in your name and in your name drive out demons and in your name perform many miracles?' Then I will tell them plainly, 'I never knew you. Away from me, you evildoers!'" (Matthew 7:21–23)

But for those who are living as the new creation, the future creation life is secure.

> Dear friends, now we are children of God, and what we will be has not yet been made known. But we know that when Christ appears, we shall be like him, for we shall see him as he is. All who have this hope in him purify themselves, just as he is pure. (1 John 3:2–3)

John explains that while we do not yet know the details of Heaven, we do know we will be like Jesus. The transformation will be over and the destination reached! The journey will be complete. Nothing will start in Heaven that had not already begun here. The eternal life of God is born in us on earth. We become more like Jesus while here on earth, will be fully like Him after death, and we will continue on through eternity. Heaven starts here. The journey into eternity starts right now.

> The one who keeps God's commands lives in him, and he in them. And this is how we know that he lives in us: We know it by the Spirit he gave us. (1 John 3:24)

If we do not know and comprehend the eternal life of God now, the eternity that we experience after death will have worse pain and emptiness. If we do know and comprehend and are partakers of the divine nature of God while alive, the eternity that we transition into after death becomes one of moving from an imperfect ecosystem to a perfect ecosystem. This is the disruption of the cross. If we do not know God and enjoy Him on earth, we won't suddenly enjoy Him in Heaven. If there is no intimacy of communion with God now, He does not commune in the future either. If there is no communication with God now, there can be no communication with Him in the future.

The post-resurrection life of Jesus gives us an indication of how the future identity will look. Jesus had a mind and body, but He could move through closed doors and travel in space and time. His identity remained the same, and He was able to identify His disciples. His recognition capacity pre-resurrection and post-resurrection remained the same. He ate with people and interacted with them. But Jesus was alive in a dimension far exceeding the dimension we can comprehend. In this dimension, the limits of time and space, as well as the restrictions of our sinful nature, are gone. Here, we will completely live out the identity we now long for in our innermost being.

The future creation is not some ghostly levitation in space. The realm of the spirit has physical properties. The spiritual system is similar to the physical except with different components. All we long for now—peace, a perfect environment, and end to all suffering—will be found in our new home. Liberation awaits the new creation.

> We know that the whole creation has been groaning as in the pains of childbirth right up to the present time. The future creation, heaven, is portrayed as a place of perfection that man is wired to experience. It is not a place of suspended animation where we do nothing, but it is an active creation, more active than the current! (Romans 8:22)

> I did not see a temple in the city, because the Lord God Almighty and the Lamb are its temple. The city does not need the sun or the moon to shine on it, for the glory of God gives it light, and the Lamb is its lamp. The nations will walk by its light, and the kings of the earth will bring their splendor into it. On no day will its gates ever be shut, for there will be no night there. The glory and honor of the nations will be brought into it. (Revelation 21:22–26)

The original creation mandate will be lived out in the future creation. If sin had not entered the world, the world would have remained the original creation. God's mandate for human beings to fill the earth, multiply, and live a God-centered life in and through the Spirit will be established in the future creation. There will be vibrant life in the future creation. The blessing to Adam and the mandate to him will be fulfilled. Life will be as it would have been if Adam and Eve had not sinned. Isaiah talks about this:

> "See, I will create new heavens and a new earth. The former things will not be remembered, nor will they come to mind. ... They will build houses and dwell in them; they will plant vineyards and eat their fruit. ... The wolf and the lamb will feed together, and the lion will eat straw like the ox, and dust will be the serpent's food. They will neither harm nor destroy on all my holy mountain," says the Lord. (Isaiah 65:17, 21, 25)

Life in the future creation will be just as it exists now, except the "former things" of sin and its implications will not exist. We will be conscious beings of the spirit with the ability to behold God, who is spirit. We will be individuals with an identity, fully complete as children of God. The future creation will be the culmination of God's ultimate strategy.

> All who have this hope in him purify themselves, just as he
> is pure. (1 John 3:3)

The hope of perfection in the future creation empowers the child of God to pursue perfection in the new creation without fear. Endurance and perseverance are demonstrations of our hope for what awaits us.

God did not create a kingdom that started with humanity, nor will it end with humanity. The kingdom of God is like God Himself, existing from eternity to eternity. The original creation, the fallen creation, the new creation, and the future creation must be seen in the context of the kingdom of God, which existed before all of these.

The beauty of the earth existed before sin. God created the beauty of nature, and He will restore all that He created to its original state. We may think the sunrise in a cloudless sky is awesome, but we cannot comprehend the beauty that will be revealed in the future creation where there is no need for the sun. The divine light will blow us away! God sees a single continuum from the original to the fallen to the new to the future. In God's kingdom, these are not disconnected segments of human history.

> I pray that the eyes of your heart may be enlightened
> in order that you may know the hope to which he has
> called you, the riches of his glorious inheritance in his
> holy people, and his incomparably great power for us who
> believe. (Ephesians 1:18–19)

We think that the present must get bigger and better for us to understand the future. The cross of Christ gives birth to a completely opposite perspective. The Spirit of God takes the Word of God and transforms our minds so that we see the bigger picture, the grandness of the inheritance, and the awesome hope of the kingdom. The clearer and grander our view of the future becomes, the better our perspective of the present.

The future creation is also about another kingdom: the kingdom of the Enemy.

> "Then he will say to those on his left, 'Depart from me, you who are cursed, into the eternal fire prepared for the devil and his angels.'" (Matthew 25:41)

We were not meant for hell, or eternal separation from God. Our destination is not supposed to be eternal fire. This is the destination of the Enemy and those who follow him. The Enemy has sold us the lie that God made hell for us. Jesus was clear when He specified for whom the eternal fire was prepared—the rebellious devil and his angels.

The Enemy and his army will be defeated, and they will forever be condemned for one reason—insubordination. Satan tried to become like God and to be above God. He did not want to accept authority.

Our future follows the Enemy into his future when we refuse to accept the disruption of the cross of Christ. The Enemy's plan is simply to take as many with him as possible. The cross, therefore, offers the exact opposite of hell—eternity spent with God in His kingdom. In the new creation, we experience the defeat of the Enemy through the cross. He will have no place in the future creation, so we fight a defeated foe whose destination is eternal separation from God.

> When the perishable has been clothed with the imperishable, and the mortal with immortality, then the saying that is written will come true: "Death has been swallowed up in victory." "Where, O death, is your victory? Where, O death, is your sting?" The sting of death is sin, and the power of sin is the law. But thanks be to God! He gives us the victory through our Lord Jesus Christ. (1 Corinthians 15:54–57)

The cross of Jesus places us in a war zone. However, we do not fight *for* victory but *from* a place of victory. Our fight demonstrates the victory that Jesus achieved over the Enemy on the cross. The Enemy will be physically removed in the future creation, but the demonstration of victory is manifested in the present through us in the new creation. The historical reality of the Enemy being crushed is demonstrated through the overcoming lifestyle of the child of God in the present new creation. We cannot be part of a kingdom in the future if we are in collaboration with the Enemy in the present. We cannot be having a lifestyle of flirting with the Enemy in the present and hope to live in a love relationship with God in the future. As much as history defines the present, the present defines the future.

The Enemy's final destination has present implications for Christians. We cannot live a defeated life now and hope for victory in the future. Biblical Christianity does not work that way. If we do not manifest the victory achieved on the cross in the new creation, we will not experience the consequences of that victory in the future creation. We cannot live a life with the Enemy in total control and then after death suddenly live a life free from his control. If the Enemy controls us in the present creation, we will live with him for eternity. We cannot be in one kingdom on earth and in another kingdom after death.

Death is only a gateway from one body to another. There is no identity transformation after death. The opportunity to change identities is available only here.

If we do not enjoy God here, we will not enjoy God after death.

If we do not seek God here, we will not see God after death.

If we are not in awe of God here, we will not experience the awe of God in the future creation.

If we do not delight in holiness here, we will not see God's holiness in the future creation.

If we do not experience the testimony of the spirit here, we will not recognize God after death.

If we do not hear God here, we will not hear God in the future creation.

If God is a stranger to us here, He will continue to be a stranger in the future creation.

Take the Next Step: A Personal Note

The journey of life is a great teacher, if we allow ourselves to learn as we live. I know what it means to be ignored by friends, and I also know what it means to be adored by friends. It is incredible to live a life where neither defines identity.

I know what it means to not know how I will pay the monthly bills for my family, and I also know how to live where money is of no concern. It is incredible to live a life knowing "financial freedom" is just a fallacy when God becomes our Father.

I know what it means to lose a job with a family to support, and I also know how it feels to have the responsibility that I support many families' jobs. It is incredible to live a life knowing that it is the support of God that matters most.

I know the pain of seeing my kids make the wrong decisions only to learn the hard way for making right decisions. I also know that I was a child who made wrong decisions. It is incredible to live a life knowing the Father who held my hand is the same One who holds the hands of my own children.

As a son, teenager, and student, as an employee and employer, and as a husband and father, I have faced staggering challenges that words cannot describe. But through it all, I have kept sight of the fact that I am on this journey of knowing Christ.

Now, I want to officially invite you to begin the journey of this dimension invasion with me.

The most incredible decision that we can make is to walk through life with God Himself. He has done His part to take residence in us, and the cross of Jesus is the evidence. But we are our own worst enemies. Our minds have been programmed into paradigms about God that prevent us from experiencing His life in us.

You may consider the life I have written about in this book as just some mystical mythology. For just a moment, try giving it the benefit of the doubt with a deeper look. If the cosmic vacuum is a reality in your life and you are seeking internally, wondering if there is something more to life than this, try taking these next steps. While science seeks and demands evidence, the question for you is: Do you want to see proof of historical evidence, or do you want to become the present evidence to a historical reality?

+ The first call to action is to decide to pursue God.

Hopefully this book has sparked a paradigm of spirituality in you—one where you seek God not for what He gives, but because spiritual communion is what you are designed for. As we have repeatedly stated, the chief end of mankind is intimacy with the Father. Once you experience this personally, you will see and agree. But you first need to make a personal decision. I am not asking you to "pray and accept Christ," change your religion, or go to church. I am asking you to decide for yourself to seek the God of the Bible. Decide to seek only Him for a time. We are all seeking something anyway, so why not seek Someone who could actually transform your life?

I will forewarn you, however, before you make this decision. There is going to be pain. When you experience God and you also fall into the lure of the sinful nature, there is going to be a new grief inside you that is painful. I am not talking about a moral guilt but the pain of grieving a Person. The principle of suffering, death, and life is hard until you begin to start experiencing the life of victory *after* the suffering and death. The Enemy is going to keep whispering in your ear that the suffering is not worth it and to give this up. So whenever this happens—and it will happen—read Psalm 51. King David wrote these words as a plea of repentance. Remember, repentance is a lifestyle. God's grace alone will keep you on the road of transformation.

Unlike Adam and Eve, we have one of the greatest privileges of denying the Enemy and experiencing real life. There is nothing on this side of Heaven that can rightly put into words the explosion of God that will happen inside you when you apply the principle of death birthing life. Whether it is the grief of giving in to what your body wants or your experience of overcoming your self-destructive triggers, the spiritual communion you will have is worth the pursuit of God.

Experiencing the dimension invasion and the co-existence of God and mankind is what you were designed to experience. But in time, you will be transformed to a radical life of experiencing and expressing God.

+   The second call to action is to get a Bible.

Personally, I like the New International Version, but the most important point of the version or translation is to get one you can best read and understand. Biblegateway.com is a great resource to check out all available versions. But it does not matter whether it is a physical or digital Bible. The advantage of an app or an online Bible is that no one is going to know what you are reading. You can keep your quest private. Your identity is not defined by flaunting a Bible anyway.

Seek God to experience Him inside you to the point where you will not be ashamed of the gospel. But don't try to force this. I promise you—life will burst forth if you continue to seek Him.

Please do not try to commit to an annual reading plan at this point. Start simple with the gospel of John or the book of Acts or Romans. And when I say read the Bible, I am actually saying to consume the Bible for breakfast, lunch, and dinner—and any time you are able to read in between.

When I started my own pursuit of God, there were no online versions yet. I was ashamed to take a Bible out in public in front of my friends. So I would write out Scriptures on paper. At breaks, while traveling, or whenever I had a chance to read on my own, I would pull out those pieces of paper and read. A mind saturated with the Word dilutes every influence of the world and makes the spiritual dimension a cognitive reality.

Don't worry if you don't understand everything you read at first. Try not to read through your usual filters of any previous religious, denominational, or positional paradigms you may have. Read the Bible for what it is and what it says, not for what you thought it said, what you think it is supposed to say, or what someone told you it says. We read things all the time in many settings we don't quite understand at first, but we all know pressing through can be one of the best decisions we ever make to learn new truths.

Receive the words like a child reading a Father's letter, for this is exactly what God intended.

If you have been spending time taking in any media of any kind—binge-watching TV, talk radio, video games, social media, or even porn, make sure you spend more time reading the Word than taking in media. Resolve this in your mind. The time you spend in God's Word should be more than taking in any of the religious or nonreligious media. This is a foundational principle of the new creation. Being saturated with the Word is a constant. Practice the presence of the Father—daily moments where you spend time with God exclusively where your thoughts are overwhelmed by His thoughts. Make practicing the presence of the Father a 24/7 experience.

> "For my thoughts are not your thoughts, neither are your ways my ways," declares the Lord. "As the heavens are

higher than the earth, so are my ways higher than your
ways and my thoughts than your thoughts. As the rain and
the snow come down from heaven, and do not return to it
without watering the earth and making it bud and flourish,
so that it yields seed for the sower and bread for the eater,
so is my word that goes out from my mouth: It will not
return to me empty, but will accomplish what I desire and
achieve the purpose for which I sent it." (Isaiah 55:8 –11)

Right now as you breathe, there is an incredible exchange of oxygen and carbon dioxide happening inside you. When you read the Word of Life, there is an incredible dimension invasion happening inside you. In this, we experience the miracle of supernatural life. Keep taking in the Word, and the miracle of life will follow. God's Word "will accomplish what I desire and achieve the purpose for which I sent it" in you.

Modern-day Pharisees still quote what Jesus told the prostitute in John 8, "Go and sin no more," but we must never forget what happened first. The men brought her to Jesus! The religion of Christianity asks people to straighten out their external behavior without first bringing them to experience Jesus. Experiencing Him will bring us to have a relationship, and therefore lose religion. When you seek Jesus first, you will gain relationship, and therefore religion will leave you. When you encounter Jesus inside you beyond mere belief, His transformation will enable you to "go and sin no more."

You don't tell a mango tree to bear mango fruit; it just does. When you and I daily spend time with Jesus, when we encounter Jesus inside us, I promise you He will guide you in whatever steps you need to take. When He does tell you what to do, you will be enabled and empowered to do so. We will be enabled to say like Jesus, "Not my will, but yours be done, heavenly Father."

There is no need to join the hypocrisy of following what the Pharisees around you tell you to do or not do. Just be intentional in filling your mind with the Word of God. When you encounter this Jesus, when He fills the cosmic vacuum inside you, when you cognitively realize you have been adopted as a son or daughter into the kingdom of your Father, you *will* live like Jesus!

My objective is to take you to the Person. Imperfect people take imperfect people to the perfect Person so He will perfect them. My goal is to take you to "the way and the truth and the life" (John 14:6). He will take it from there. As there is one perfect Person, there is one perfect Book, the Bible. Pick up the perfect Book that this imperfect book is directing you to.

Finally, your current profile does not matter. You may be in Hollywood or Bollywood or in the worst place you have ever been in your life. You may be on Wall Street, or you may be living on the street. You may be in the Silicon Valley, or you may be in the darkest valley of your life.

No matter who you are, where you've been, what you've become, or what you have done, take the next step and start the journey of a life of disruption where Jesus Christ will bring you to gain relationship and lose religion!

Printed in the United States
By Bookmasters